RAY MOORE.

SIRENS OVER THE VALLEY

Also by Rachael Ann Webb:

From Caerau to the Southern Cross

SIRENS OVER THE VALLEY

by Rachael Ann Webb

Rachel Ann Webb

ALUN BOOKS
3 Crown Street, Port Talbot, West Glamorgan

Photoset, printed and bound in Great Britain by
WBC Ltd, Bristol and Maesteg

FOREWORD

Rachael Bowen was born in 1903, into the comfortable world of the Edwardian middle classes, but soon her barrister father's illness and the hospital bills it led to, left the Bowens comparatively poor, and they had to move from the comforts of Swansea to a humbler home in Blackwood. When her father died (on the morning of the Senhenydd explosion), the family—now mother, two sons and three daughters—moved again, to the Maesteg area, and began their long bitter struggle to survive.

As she grew older, Rachel began to take her part in helping to support the family; she trained as a nurse and a land girl, and later spent a perilous few months in London, working as a maid in what proved to be the headquarters of a gang of White Slavers. After a narrow escape from this danger, she spent a while as an apprentice lace-mender in Dorset; then, on her return home she was swept off her feet by Ivor Webb, a handsome young miner, and duly became Mrs. Webb and, later, the mother of two lively children.

However, it was the period of the Depression, and when Pearl, the younger child, was about a year old, the Webbs decided to emigrate to Australia, 'the land of opportunity'. (Rachel's elder sister had married an Australian soldier, and they planned to live near her.) Ivor went first, to prepare a home for them, and Rachel and the children followed a few months later.

Sadly, when they arrived at their new home, they found that Australia was having its own Depression; work was hard to come by, and Ivor had only been able to find the most rudimentary shelter for them. Still, Rachel settled down, with her usual ingenuity and determination, to the task of making a new life, and despite all the hardships, the intense heat and even the initial hostility of their neighbours (who were afraid for their own jobs), they turned their tin shack into a home, and their neighbours into good friends.

v

ONE

Before I left England I was supposed to have gone into hospital for treatment to repair the damage I had suffered after the birth of my little girl, and while I was staying with my mother a letter came, telling me to report to the hospital. When I did present myself there, I told them that I was sailing for Australia in a fortnight, and the specialist said that he was sorry to hear that I was going there, because it was the last country in the world I should be going to. Then he told me that the operation I needed was urgent, but if I had it, I would not be allowed to travel for at least a year. At that I said I would not be able to stay, I had to go to Australia because my husband was alone out there, and I had two children, so I would leave the operation and have it when I got out to Australia.

The specialist went on to explain that if I insisted on going, they would have to put me in a linen harness. This harness weighed the equivalent of six yards of calico, and had to be stepped into; it came up over my body and my shoulders to take the weight off my body and legs (and I still carry the marks of its weight on my body today.) I did not tell my mother in detail of the conversation I had had with the specialist, because I did not want to worry her, but I did tell her that I had promised the doctor that I would have the operation when I got to Australia.

All I knew at that point, of course, was that I was voyaging to the land of perpetual sunshine; the advertisements called it "the land of milk and honey" and urged "Come to the land of opportunities, the golden west". No mention was made of the fact that Australia was suffering the aftermath of the Great War and going through a depression that meant that there was no work, but there *was* starvation and suicide. Nor did I know that my husband was trapped in the "great Australian bush", or that we were going to find it hard to buy a loaf of bread, let alone cover the cost of medical treatment. (The operation which I would have had free in Britain, would have cost at least a thousand pounds in

1

Australia.) I wore the harness for six years in that tremendous heat, where the temperature often rose to a hundred and twenty four in the shade; and when I could at last afford the twenty-five shillings needed just for knocking on the doctor's door, I told him about my health, but did not mention the harness I was wearing, or the fact that I needed an operation. The doctor said to me, 'Whatever possessed you, Mrs. Webb, to come to such a hole as this—you, of all people, to bury yourself away in the bush.'

'The doctor advised us to take our two children to a warmer climate,' I told him. 'And as my sister had married an Australian during the war and now lives in Northampton, we thought this was the ideal place to come to. We had no idea of the hardships we would encounter, but we do have one consolation: our children have thrived in the sunshine.'

I went on to explain that after six years we had learned to overcome the hardships and had grown to love the country (except for the heat!). And as for the people, though at first they had been hostile to us, by now we were surrounded by kind and and caring friends; our very poverty and hardship had brought us all closer together in a bond of friendship that no money could buy. 'It will be very hard when I have to say goodbye to "my little grey home in the west", and all these people I have learned to love,' I finished.

However, the doctor told me that unless I returned to my native land, he would give me just two months to live. 'And although the sun has been good to your little boy,' he added, 'you will have to take your girl home. This intense heat has weakened her heart, and she could develop epileptic fits.' After that I had no choice but to tell my husband that we would have to go back to Wales.

Now we had to think of a means of getting the money to go back, as well as to provide warm clothing for the voyage. We still had twenty-five pounds in the bank (my sister-in-law had sent it), and there was a little saved up in a tin box nailed under the floor of our home, which Mrs. M'Gee had given me for nursing her children. We also had four hundred laying hens, but there was no sale for the eggs, because in that high temperature they were partly cooked as they were laid, and we had no facilities for keeping them cool. We had no furniture that was fit to sell, and no other assets to sell except the horse and sulky, and the cow. We sold the cow and the sulky, but we hoped to keep the horse, because Ivor would need it after I had gone home with the

2

children. (Ivor would be giving up our home and going to live with Viv and Edwina Husband, where he would work for his keep.) To our dismay we found that even with the sale of the horse, we could only raise enough money to pay for one full fare and one half fare, and there was no way we could find the half fare for our other little one.

I made my application for a passport, but this was a further difficulty. It had been very easy to get a passage out to Australia, but once one was there, the Australian government made it very hard to leave the country. Every obstacle was put in my way. First I had to send a medical certificate when applying to leave, and I had to sign clearance papers to prove that I didn't owe the government any money. Next they had to be satisfied that all the questions on the form were answered correctly, and I had to have witnesses to prove that I would be leaving without owing money to a single person in Australia, and that I had no complaints against Australia or Australians. Then I had to furnish three references to show that I was of good character, so I got one from the bank manager, one from the police and one from the chapel minister.

Still my greatest problem was to find money to pay for the other child; even after we sold Ivor's horse, there was no way that I could get enough. I was in a terrible predicament since it was impossible for me to go home and leave one child behind. There was only one thing I could do, and though I prayed long and hard to God to show me another way to take both my children back, He didn't help me raise money. I had no-one else to turn to, so I falsified the ages of my children on my "application for passage" form. By law I was allowed to take one child free of charge *if* it was under the age of two, and *if* I paid half fare for the other child. So I said that Pearl was under two years old (she was actually almost seven) and though I had to pay for Jack, I lowered his age too, so that it wouldn't look too odd; if anyone said they looked older, I planned to say that they looked old for their age!

Eventually my passport arrived, just two weeks before my two months was up. As a Christian the deception over the children's ages still worried me, but I felt sure that God would understand, and at last the day came when I had to leave my husband and the little home we had shared together; we had been very happy there, even if it was very humble. Ivor was taking my two galahs and all the chickens to Edwina's farm, and Jimmy the emu was going to

3

Perth Zoo. We did leave our pet lizard, which was a fly lizard—he lived only on flies, so we had no fear of him starving to death. I had not said goodbye to anyone because I had had no time; the six weeks had left me just enough time to make some warmer clothes for my children, ready for the cooler climate of Wales. Since I couldn't say goodbye to the Davidsons, the M'Gees or the Hendleys, I left it to Ivor to make my apologies and tell them that I couldn't bear to say goodbye. It was even harder still to say goodbye to my sister Emily and her four children.

On the morning of my departure Emily and her children walked with me to the railway station, and it was a big strain holding back the tears as we sat waiting for the train. I thought of all the friends we had made—but worst of all I thought of how I would have to leave my husband to the mercy of that wild life. Ivor himself was happy in it, because it was a man's country, and the freedom of the life out there suited him; he loved Australia. He had a private word that morning with Jack and Pearl, and Jack told me later that Daddy had told him, 'When Mammy is better, ask her to bring you back to Australia, and you and Pearl shall have a pony, and we will have a nice stone house to live in.'

Ivor had given me a letter to take home with me, which I was instructed to take to his solicitor. I was to act on my husband's behalf, and all the property and cash which had been left to him by his father, were to be handed over to me; I was given power to sell property in his name. Ivor told me that if, when I was well enough, I wanted to go back, he would build us a stone house which would protect us from the heat. However, I made no promises—I couldn't promise to return to Australia because I didn't know how things would turn out, I would just have to wait and see.

The train steamed out of Northampton, and I sat back in my seat and cried. (The children couldn't understand why I was crying when they were so excited.) Then we arrived in Geraldton, where we had to stay the night, since the train for Perth didn't leave until the morning. My cabin trunk had gone on ahead, so I only had my hand luggage, and we found a room for the night, close to the railway station. After we had settled into our room, I took the children for a walk along the coast; Geraldton is a sea port. It was very hot, and we sat on some rocks, facing the sea, hoping for a sea breeze to cool us down. There seemed to be no-one about, and we were alone, which gave me time to think. I was

4

happy to be going home, and looking forward to seeing my mother and all the family and friends I had left behind when I emigrated to Australia. I was also looking forward to having the operation that would free me from the torture of the harness that I wore next to my skin. And yet the joy of returning home was marred by the heartbreak of leaving my husband, and perhaps losing all that we had worked for so hard. It seemed that all that hard graft could have been in vain, and I was sad too that I was leaving Emily, Jim and the four children I loved so much. The children soon realised why I was crying, and said to me, 'Don't cry, Mummy, we'll soon see Daddy again.'

It was getting dark now, and I saw a man and woman come and sit on the rocks nearby; I could hear the murmur of their voices, but not exactly what was being said. Back at our lodgings I asked the landlady for three cups of cocoa. (I knew I would not be able to afford to buy food for us, so I had packed some cakes and sandwiches before leaving home.) As usual, the children knelt down and said their prayers, and I knelt down with them, but when I got up off my knees, I was surprised to see someone standing in the doorway. It was the landlady, and she had quite a little crowd of people standing round her. 'What are you doing, kneeling down at the side of your bed?' she asked. I looked at her in surprise, then realised from her remark that this was something they were not used to in her house.

'Why, we were saying our prayers,' I said. Next morning, as we sat down to breakfast, a woman said to me, 'How do you like our water?' 'It tastes all right,' I replied, and the woman told me that it was condensed sea water, the result of an experiment, and had only recently been laid on. I told her that it tasted very good, but I had never heard of sea water being condensed for drinking—it was something that I learned on my last day in Australia. After that we went to the railway station, where the "Southern Cross" stood waiting, while the engine was being moved from the front of the train to the back, ready to take us back down to Perth.

I knew I would have to go to Australia House to collect my passports, and I was very worried because I thought they would ask to see the children and so find out that I had falsified their ages on the form. Still, I was desperate now, and I didn't care. If they found out, then all they could do would be to refuse me passage and sent me home. Indeed, I think I would have been relieved if they *had* sent me back, because of my worry and anxiety at the

5

thought of the fifteen thousand miles of travel I faced, with two lively children to guard. I felt sure that the strain was showing on my face, and I know that I felt twenty years older after signing the forms.

There were two young girls in my compartment, who were travelling just a short way down the line, as well as a tall, sad-faced woman of about fifty who hurried me into the carriage with my children and my luggage, and then took up her position at the window and leaned out to speak to an elderly man who was standing on the platform. It was obvious that she was saying goodbye to him, for the tears were streaming down her face. We took our seats at the furthest end of the carriage, sad that there was no-one to wish us a safe journey; then we waited patiently for the train to leave the station. As soon as that happened, the woman hurried across to the opposite side of the carriage, where she stood waving frantically to what looked to me like empty fields—until I spotted a man and a teenage boy waving back to her, and blowing kisses. They were standing in a potato patch at the side of the line. When the train went out of sight of the men, she sat back in her seat and wept bitterly. I looked around the compartment, embarrassed by her sorrow, to see what facilities there were for our comfort; the compartment was to be our home for the next three days and nights.

The seats were slightly wider than the carriage seats in Britain, and stretched across the width of the compartment on one side; on the other, the seat went three quarters of the way across, and this allowed for a small door which led into a little room in which there was a toilet and a wash basin (with cold water only) in which to wash one's hands. Outside the carriage window, on the offside, was a canvas bag, attached underneath the window, which held drinking water. I knew the nights would be very cold, because it was the cool season, and although the days were hot, the nights were chilly, so I looked around to see how we could keep warm. The girls in the compartment told me that if I lifted up my seat, I would find pillows and blankets underneath, and we would find it all quite comfortable; they left the train at the next stop.

All through the journey there seemed to be no life at all, and every mile we travelled was the same, just dry, barren land. There was no restaurant on this train, and passengers travelling to Perth had to carry food with them, so I had bought sandwiches, cakes, biscuits and fruit, and hoped that that would be enough to see us through the next four days. (We had a day's travel by bus after leaving the train). The woman had calmed down by now, and was reading a newspaper; she read out loud to me, "Murdered for Sixpence", and added, 'Fancy, a young man murdered and all they found on him was sixpence! This country is hell itself!' With that, she lapsed back into silent sorrow. Her outburst had startled me, and I thought, if a man could be murdered for sixpence, what chance would I have, a woman travelling alone and carrying as much money as I was (I was taking it to London House, Perth, to pay for our passage.)

The woman said to me, 'Be careful with your handbag, my dear, keep the strap over your arm. Where are you going, my dear?'

'To England,' I said. She made no real attempt at conversation, just uttered a snatched remark here and there, and she made no comment when I mentioned England, but just sat back in her seat, too absorbed in her own sorrow to note what I said. I did not volunteer any more remarks, but just sat quietly, respecting her grief. Then suddenly she terrified me by leaping out of her seat and leaning over me. 'What did you say?' she shouted, 'where did you say you were going?'

The children, who were one on each side of me, snuggled up to me as if they too had had a shock. Again the woman demanded to know where I was going, and stood there, towering over me. Falteringly, I said, 'To England.' I thought the woman was demented, and I thought too about the man murdered for sixpence, and remembered the cord around my neck, to which was attached the little bag, tucked inside my blouse, which held the money to pay for our passports, plus a little over to see us safely back to Wales. Then the woman sank back in her seat, covered her face with her hands, and said, 'I thought that was what you said, England, England.' When she had composed herself sufficiently, she exclaimed, 'Oh you lucky, lucky girl. England, England, oh beloved, beautiful England!' Then she began to tell me the reason for her sorrow.

'Did you see that man and boy standing in the potato patch? That is all we have to live on—we have lived on potatoes for weeks and weeks. And those were my husband and son. We too came out from England some years ago. I have another daughter and son, but unfortunately they both married out here. We had a good business in England, but we sold everything to come out to the "land of perpetual sunshine and prosperity", and set up

7

business here in Geraldton instead. Now this cursed land has robbed us of everything.' She was very bitter. 'Now,' she went on, 'we live in a tin shanty, and all we've had to live on for some time has been potatoes, and we wouldn't have had those if my husband and son hadn't planted and grown them themselves. Last night, when my husband and I sat on the rocks, we saw you and your children. We sat there to say our goodbyes, and as we gazed out across the ocean, the only words we could bring outselves to say were, 'It's all for England.' You see, I am leaving my husband and son, and going, God knows where, far away to a lonely place. I answered an advertisement which described the place as miles from anywhere, and I am to be housekeeper to a lonely man. I don't want to go, but there's no alternative. Either I starve in a shack with my husband and son, or I go to this job and have good food and good wages. I've promised that every penny I earn will be saved, and when I have enough money for the three of us, then we will wipe the dust of this godforsaken country off our feet and sail for England.'

During the night the train stopped, for the first time since letting the girls off, and the woman, Mrs. Rose, gathered up her belongings and wished me a safe journey. Once again she warned me. 'If anyone speaks to you, don't even tell them you are going to England or they will know you are carrying money. Be careful.' She stepped down from the train on to a wooden square, placed there for her to alight on to, because there was no platform—and no station, either. The driver of the train guided her, with his lantern, to a little tin shed. There was neither sound nor sign of life, and she stood there, a woman alone in the wilds of Australia, waiting for her employer to meet her, as the train puffed away.

The train went on its way in complete darkness; there was not a glimmer of light in any direction, and not a sound to be heard, not even of cattle or sheep, nor a railway station along the way to break the monotony. We were indeed travelling through barren wastes. The two little ones were cosily tucked up and fast asleep, and I prepared myself for bed. (This was a much more comfortable journey than the one we had when we first came to Australia, when we had travelled over the Wangan hills in the utility carriages, without even a blanket to cover us.) We had brought Pearl's dolly pram and dolls with us, and next day the children amused themselves with those, and I read stories to them as well, to keep them happy.

On the fourth day we arrived in Perth, and we then had to find our way to London House; once again, after putting my anxieties to the back of my mind during the journey, I was face to face with reality. Happily, though the children were very excited, they were very well behaved, and I had no problem with them. I prayed silently that everybody would be all right and we would be allowed to go to England, and so it was. I was given my passport, with my photograph, which was on the inside cover, duly stamped, and inside was written "Travelling alone with boy aged six and girl, aged two". The officials were very kind and helpful to me, and I knew in myself that whatever sin I might have committed in my false statement, I was embarking on this long voyage with my little ones with my Lord's blessing.

We spent a little time looking around the shops in Perth. It was a lovely morning; the air was soft and warm, without too much heat. I saw a pair of shoes in a shop window, and longed to buy them, but first I had to do a little mental arithmetic to see if I had enough money to spare to pay for them. The shoes I was wearing were the only shoes I had, and they had been throw-outs from Stokes's shop, bought for a few pennies. Each shoe had doubled up like a sandwich through the intense heat, so I had put them to stand in a bowl of water at home; when the leather was soft and pliable, I filled each shoe full of wheat (grown by ourselves) and left them standing in the water until the wheat had swollen and pressed the shoes into shape. Now I was able to wear them; the problem with the other pair of shoes in the window was that they were size two and my shoe size was three and a half, but I took a chance and brought them so that I would have a change of shoes for the long voyage.

Then we took a bus to Fremantle and looked around for a place to sleep that night. In the Fremantle docks I saw a small shop, with a card in the window, and when I went inside there were some seamen sitting drinking tea. I asked the man behind the counter if I could have a bed for the night, at which the man seemed surprised, and stared at me, but he told me the price of a room, and said it was payable in advance. I paid him, and he said, 'Follow me.' We went down a stone passage and turned into a room on the right, a narrow room, no more than six feet wide, with white-limed walls. In it were two single beds, head to foot against the wall. There was no other furniture in the room, but the beds were nice and clean, with white sheets and white counterpanes.

(I needed to be near the ship, in case we overslept in the morning; it was my great fear that we would miss the boat.)

I took the children out then to buy a postcard to send to Daddy, to tell him we had arrived safely. After that we looked round the Fremantle shops and I bought a drink each for us, and a little something to eat; I couldn't afford to buy a meal. Then I made enquiries as to whether the ship had arrived, and was told that it had docked, so we went along to see it. It was a beautiful, majestic three-funnelled liner, standing high in the water, right next to the dock. There was a man sitting at the foot of the gang way, and he told me that he was a watchman, noting everyone going on and off the ship, because they had to look out for stowaways.

'Every ship that leaves Fremantle,' he said, 'has to check every passport thoroughly, to prevent stowaways from sneaking on to the ship, and tomorrow morning when passengers are boarding, there will be crowds of people on the dock mixing with the passengers, trying to get on board, because they are desperate to get back to "dear old England", but have no money to pay the fare. They come every day, hoping to smuggle themselves aboard unseen.'

I told him that we had come to see the ship that was to be our home for the next six weeks, and he asked me how far we had come. When I told him that we had come almost seven hundred miles, he was surprised to hear that I had travelled all those miles alone with my children. Then I showed him my embarkation papers, and said that we had booked a room here at the docks; at that he said, 'I hope you haven't paid for your room.'

'Yes,' I said. 'I had to pay in advance.' He told me to go back and get my luggage from the room because there was no need for me to sleep there—I could come aboard and sleep on the ship. So I went back to the little shop, collected my luggage and told the man that I wouldn't be needing the room after all. I had to forfeit the money already paid, but I was glad to get away from there, because I had a feeling that the place was not safe for me and the children.

I went back to the ship, and an officer helped me and the children aboard. There were very few people on the ship yet, but I met a woman there with her own two children, who was travelling home from the East. She came over to speak to me and we formed a nice friendship that lasted throughout the voyage. We were shown to our cabin by one of the ship's officers, who made us

10

welcome; as this ship was returning to England, it was not as crowded as the ship on our outward journey, and we had a cabin to ourselves.

Next morning we went up on deck to watch the embarkation of the other passengers, who were not due to arrive until ten o'clock. It was a lovely feeling to know that all the anxieties, the goodbyes and the long journey were behind me, and I felt like a bird that has been let out of its cage; I longed to set foot on Australian soil again for the last time. All the promenade deck had mesh wire around the rails, so there was no fear of the children overboard, and I asked the little ones if they would be especially good, and stay on board exactly where I would leave them, while I went to the post office to send another letter to Daddy, to tell him we were safely aboard the liner. They said they would stay, and since I knew my children's word was their bond, I knew I could safely leave them. I would only be away for about ten minutes at most. However I also asked the watchman to please be sure not to let my children come off the boat.

'Don't worry, Madam,' he said. 'I don't move off my seat, and I will send them back if they attempt to come down.'

It was wonderful to feel free of so much responsibility for just a few minutes. I scribbled a message to my husband, posted it, and returned to the ship. As I walked up the gangway, I asked the watchman if the children had attempted to come down, and he said, 'No, Madam, they haven't.' However, when I got back on board, the children were nowhere to be seen, and when I asked the officers if *they* had seen them, no-one had done so. Now I was afraid again, remembering the time they had been lost in the bush, and began to visualise the ship leaving with me on board and my children running round Fremantle looking for me. Then a young officer approached me, and I asked him if he had seen my children.

'Now, Madam,' he said, 'calm down, nobody is going to steal your little ones from you, they are safely on board somewhere and we'll find them. The ship is being searched, and we won't sail until we have found your children.'

Still there was no sign of them aboard, in spite of the assurances that they had not gone ashore—and then there they were, walking towards me hand in hand with the captain who said, 'Madam, I congratulate you, you have charming children.' I asked them why they had left the rail, and they said that the captain had seen them

11

waiting for me, and taken them for a little walk. For the whole of the voyage after that, the officer who had helped me look for the children would whisper every time he passed me, 'What a woman, losing her children aboard our lovely liner!' It seemed that the captain had introduced my children to the engineers, and they became their mascots, spending hours in the company of the officers and engineers when they were off duty.

TWO

On this voyage the departure was not the joyful occasion that it had been when we were boarding the ship to come from Britain to Australia. There were no streamers and no band playing "God be with you till we meet again", and though there were crowds on the quay, there were no sad farewells. I remarked on this to the officer standing beside me at the rail, and he said, 'This is the usual departure of a liner from this country. There are thousands of disillusioned Britishers who would walk back to England if there was a bridge crossing the ocean.' There were many people standing on the quay, booing and jeering at us as we pulled slowly away, and the officer explained, 'These people are here every time we come to these docks. They boo because once again they have failed to get onto the ship.'

The children chummed up with an elderly gentleman who, I discovered, was taking the round trip for his health; this was the return leg to England. He recognised my accent and commented, 'You are Welsh, aren't you? What part of Wales do you come from?'

'From Glamorgan,' I said.

He smiled and said, 'I once owned the Star Hotel in Maesteg.'

He was a very wealthy man, and had taken his manservant along with him on the trip; he told me that he had shares in goldmines in Australia and South Africa. We became good travelling companions for the whole voyage.

On the first morning at sea, I took the children into the dining room for breakfast, and we were shown to the table which was to be ours for the six week voyage. To my surprise (because on our outward journey we had all been seated around long tables) the dining room tables were small, seating four people, and the three of us were seated at a table where there also sat a snobbish young man of about thirty years of age. The liner was a one-class ship, but passengers with the means to do so could pay for better cabins above deck, and the young man was evidently one of these, but there was no difference in the dining room or the meals served

13

there. Each passenger was allotted his or her table for the whole voyage, with no picking or choosing allowed, but when this young man saw that he was to share his table with two children, he said to the steward, 'I refuse to eat at a table with children. Get me another place at once.'

The steward told him politely that he had no authority to change the positions allotted in the dining hall, and all the tables were occupied. At this the man demanded to see the captain, but instead he was referred to the purser, so he stormed from the table, saying, 'I will do that. I will not sit down to table with children.' Meanwhile the children and I went quietly on with our meal, taking no notice of the obnoxious young man and his tantrums. The steward smiled at me and said, 'Madam, any gentleman would be honoured to sit at your table, with your little ones, but don't worry, the purser will send him back with a flea in his ear.' And indeed, judging by the way he returned to the table, he had indeed been put in his place by both the captain and the purser. Although my little ones had been brought up in the bush, their table manners were far superior to his. They didn't have to be reminded to say Grace before and after meals, something that I noticed he didn't do. I only saw the young man at meal times, when I would nod at him in greeting, when he sat down at the table, but my only conversation was with my children.

We were now far out to sea, and every morning the old gentleman, Mr. Lewis, who, I learned, was eighty years old, would look out for us; being a seasoned traveller he had some very interesting stories to tell, and I had a lot to learn. When we arrived at Colombo, he insisted on taking the three of us ashore. The liner anchored a mile off shore, and boats came to it to take the passengers to land; the cost of that little trip was half a crown (12½p). So, with Jack and Pearl walking each side of Mr. Lewis and holding tightly to his hands, and me walking behind them, we went down the gangway into the boat. Mr. Lewis looked like an adoring grandfather, walking his grandchildren. As we went down the gangway, I saw that an officer stood on either side and made a note of everyone leaving the ship.

We spent the whole day ashore, and had a marvellous time, thanks to Mr. Lewis. We sat at tables by the roadside, under large umbrellas, and were served with icecream and refreshments. However, I had to restrain Mr Lewis from showering myself and my children with gifts. I told him that I didn't want the children to

14

be spoilt, because they knew that I could not afford to buy them gifts, and they didn't expect anything or ask for anything. I tried to explain that I wanted my children to love people for what they were, not for what they could give them.

As we went along, we met up with a group of passengers from our ship who seemed to be overpowered by the heat and looked quite languid. The women asked me why we looked so cool in the heat and didn't seem to be the least bit disturbed by it. (They had come from the eastern side of Australia, where the climate was cooler, nearer to that of Britain.) I told them that we didn't find it over-hot, but just comfortable, so they asked what part of Australia we came from. When I told them that we had lived almost seven hundred miles inland from Perth, within walking distance of the Calgoorlie gold fields, they murmured amongst themselves, 'No wonder they look so cool—you are used to intense heat, aren't you?'

When the children saw the water sellers in their native costume, they had to have a penny to buy a glass of water from them; this was poured from a goatskin bag hanging at the water seller's side, and for another penny the men would stand beside the children and have a photograph taken. When we arrived back on the ship that evening, I found that Pearl had a beautiful Indian bangle on her arm, a gift that Mr. Lewis had put there unknown to me. I didn't wish to encourage him to buy presents so I did not thank him, or even show him that I had seen the bangle, but I did let him know, in a nice way, that I didn't want my children to be overcome by a display of wealth, because I knew that all this would end the minute we left the ship. We were working class people and I did not want the children to get used to things they could not have.

Our next port of call was India, and the night before we docked Mr. Lewis said to me, 'You *will* be coming ashore with me tomorrow, won't you? You must be ready early, as we will be leaving first thing.' I tried to protest, but he insisted, and came looking for us in the morning, saying he wanted to go ashore, but couldn't go without us. He was wearing a silk tussore suit and a white panama hat. Jack wore shorts, with a white silk blouse and a white silk pith helmet, while Pearl had on a pale blue silk frock and a pale blue silk sun bonnet. Mr. Lewis took each child by the hand, and told me to keep close, because there would be a tremendous crush of people around the gangway, waiting to go

15

ashore. (We were seven hundred souls on board, not including the crew.)

I had difficulty in keeping close to Mr. Lewis, what with all the people crowding round, and as we went past the officers, I heard the old gentleman say, 'Myself and the two children and the missus behind.' I felt terrible, and thought 'Surely that isn't what he is allowing these people to think that I am his wife—that this old man is the father of my two lovely children!' Just then, in my embarrassment at being called his missus, I recalled Ivor's words as we walked with our two babies in their pram, one day in Wales, before we left for Australia. He had said, 'One day you'll be an old man's darling,' and I had smiled at the compliment and said to him, 'When you are an old man, I'll be an old woman too.'

We had a wonderful day ashore in India; it was even better than Ceylon. As we sat under a large umbrella out in the open, enjoying our refreshments, we were being entertained by little brown boys doing magic tricks. For a silver shilling, they would make the coin disappear, then wave their hands over Jack's ear, say "gulley, gulley" and then take the shilling from behind his ear. Jack was enthralled with them and all their magic tricks. We returned to the ship that night, tired but happy, and the children had a store of memories to keep in their minds.

Slowly we drew nearer the Red Sea, and it became unbearably hot. We were issued with sweat towels, to put around our shoulders, and were given a hard, dry ship's biscuit to nibble between meals, as well as half a large orange or other citrus fruit; these were handed around to the passengers on deck. Our hair hung limp, soaked in perspiration, which also ran down our faces. Father Neptune came aboard as we crossed the line, and we had a very entertaining evening.

We were given lifeboat drill several times during the voyage. Life jackets had been put on each bed as we came aboard, and we were trained in the use of them, so that if there was a disaster at sea, each passenger would quickly, but quietly, don his or her life jacket and proceed, also quickly and quietly, to his or her boat deck, above the promenade deck, where they would stand in their places near the life boats which hung in cradles at the side of the boat.

There was a lot of entertainment aboard; at the beginning of every voyage a committee was formed which would be responsible for entertainments and sports. Now a children's party and fancy

16

dress parade was announced, and I dressed Pearl up, putting her curls in a bun at the back of her head; she was dressed as a little old woman, with a doll in each arm, while Jack wore a borrowed long trousers and a shirt with the sleeves rolled up, with a man's flat cap (lent by one of the men). He carried a kewpie doll in one hand and pushed a pram carrying two rag dolls; the couple went as "Married Bliss" and won first prize. The prize was chocolates, and they thoroughly enjoyed taking part with the other children.

Thanks to Mr. Lewis, we had had a very happy voyage, and one day, when we had been at sea for a long time after leaving the last port, Mr. Lewis told me about his family, the first time I had ever heard him mention them. He had bought a gift for his grand-daughter who, he said, was eighteen years old, and looked like me. He took a ring box out of his pocket, and showed me a beautiful opal ring, asking if I thought she would like it. I said that I was sure she would love it, and then he asked if I would try it on for size; he put it on my finger over my wedding ring, and then, when I went to take it off, to hand it back to him, he took my hand in both of his and said, 'You mustn't take it off, it would be a shame. It looks so nice on your hand, keep it and remember me.'

I protested, saying that it was too costly a gift and he must take it home to his grand-daughter. 'I don't need a present to remember you by,' I said. 'I shall remember your kindness to me and the children, always, and our long voyage together.' I had always refused to take any gifts from him, but he said that he had wanted to give me much more, and if I did not accept the ring, he would be very hurt.

As we were passing Aden, we were standing on deck, watching the land in the distance; one of the officers who was standing nearby, told us that they had radioed back to England to announce the exact time of our passing through Aden. Then he suddenly exclaimed, and we looked towards the land, in which direction we could see a large black object coming straight towards us. It was a huge oil tanker. Something happened then, and we were all thrown on to the deck, where we lay, shaken and amazed at what had happened. The deck steward was trying to calm the passengers, while the others rushed round in confusion.

Afterwards we were told what had happened. Our ship had been alerted the day before that a ship passing Aden had disappeared with all hands, leaving no trace whatsoever, and had it not been for that alert and the careful watch kept by the crew of our boat, they would not have spotted that oil tanker in time to avert another tragedy. The tanker had been heading for the middle of our liner, and the officer said that if it had reached us, it would have cut our liner in two and we would have sunk immediately. The engineers had swung us around just in time to avoid the collision, and that was what had thrown us to the floor; only their promptness saved us, and the speed of the tanker took her past our bows with just inches to spare.

Although we had had a very good crossing, and there had not been a lot of sea sickness, I now felt rather ill, and thought I was going to have an attack of this sickness. I tried to throw it off, but after lunch, when we went to our cabin to have a rest, I explained to the children that I needed to go to sleep for a little while, and then asked them to look after each other and not to wander too far from the cabin. I fell into a heavy sleep, and must have slept for hours; when I awoke, the children were fast asleep on their bunks, and since I thought I had only slept for a little while, and now felt much better, it seemed a good opportunity to do my washing. I gathered up the clothes and made for the bathroom. It was usual to have to wait one's turn to wash in the bathroom, and I couldn't understand why there seemed to be no-one about.

When my washing was done, I took it to the large drying room set out below deck. I found an empty clothesline and began hanging out the clothes, quietly humming to myself. It was a treat to have done my washing without any hindrance. Then I heard a voice say, 'Hello, there.' It was one of the deck stewards, and I made a joke about him helping me to peg out my washing. We exchanged a few jovial remarks and I said, jokingly, 'You should have come sooner to help me with my washing. I was very lucky to have the bathroom to myself, and now all the clotheslines are empty. Where is everybody?'

At that he said, 'Young lady, do you know what time it is? It's four o'clock in the morning!'

I scuttled back to my cabin and found that the children were still asleep. We were now passing the Rock of Gibraltar; later, when we came near to England, the particular officer who was always there to give us information, said to us, 'Come on, you *must* catch your first glimpse of the White Cliffs of Dover.' There were a man and a woman standing at the rail; he was an Englishman with an Australian wife, as well as a little boy of about six years old, and now he told his wife to look up into the

18

sky and see a grey sky for the first time in her life. It was then that I realised that I had not seen a grey sky since I said goodbye to these cliffs at Dover six years before. I remembered how I had thought then that I would never see them again and had stood at the rail, heart-broken, bidding farewell to the land of my birth. Words had come into my mind then which I had spoken quietly to myself in my native Welsh:

Farewell to the land, to the moors and the mountains,
Farewell to the beautiful land of my birth.
The high mountain peaks shall no more behold me,
I go far away to the ends of the earth.

Now, after all, I was home again, to a new beginning.

THREE

Later, as I stood at the rail of the liner, with my children at my side, I told them that we were coming back to the grey skies of home. It was strange to see the sky so far above us when in Australia it had been quite low, and a lovely azure blue. At night it had often been so low that it felt as if we were in a box and the sky was a lid closing down on us in the dense, stifling heat. But I had often looked up at the Southern Cross and thought it seemed to hover above our shack as if it was there for our protection.

Now, seeing the sky such a vast distance above us gave me a sense of freedom—such as a bird must feel when it escapes from a cage—and I knew that although we had seen many lovely sights on our voyage, and visited many pretty places, we were coming back to the most beautiful country in the world. England or Wales, I knew now that these were truly the lands of opportunity, of milk and honey, the country where no-one hungers or thirsts.

Just then the bell rang for lunch-time, so we left the rail and went into the dining room. After lunch we walked around the ship until we met Mr. Lewis, and then the old gentleman and I sat and talked while the children played around us. However, my mind was not on the conversation, and several times Mr. Lewis jolted me back to earth, saying, 'You are not with us today, Rachael.'

'I just wished I had my husband, and my sister and her four lovely children, returning to England with me,' I told him. 'It saddens me to have left them behind in Australia, and I was thinking of the joy it would have been to be able to present my mother with her oldest daughter and *her* children as well as me and *my* two little ones.'

But this explanation did not satisfy Mr. Lewis, and he said, 'I have noticed a lot of care in your face lately. There is something worrying you, isn't there?'

I thought I had kept my guilty secret safely locked away during

20

the voyage, but now I found myself telling Mr. Lewis that the doctor had said I would be dead in two months if I didn't leave Australia. Then I explained that, try as we could, we had not been able to gather enough money for the full fares home, only sufficient for one and a half tickets.

'How could I leave one of my children behind?' I asked. 'Pearl had to come with me, the doctor told me that her heart had been weakened. There was only one thing I could do, and that was to bring her back as a two-year-old on a free passage. When I went to collect my passport and pay my fares, they saw my two children, but they made no comment on their size. Now I am wondering if they might query this when we disembark, and I feel a little concerned.'

Mr. Lewis was also concerned, and made me feel even worse by telling me that I had done something very wrong, but then he said, 'Don't worry about it, dear, I'll put it right.'

However, I told him that he was on no account to mention it or do anything about it, because I would be most hurt and offended if he interfered in any way.

'It is easy to be righteous when you've got everything, but what would you have done in my circumstances? My greatest sin has been committed against God, and I know I have come with *His* blessing because I put all my anxieties and misdeeds before Him and trusted in His compassion. My sin against the shipping company I can put right when my husband's property has been sold. As for your offer, you and I are like ships that pass in the night; we might never meet again, and I don't want a debt to you on my conscience. Instead, the kindness you have shown me and my little ones during the voyage shall be my memory of you in the years to come.'

We were to disembark on the following morning, but I told Mr. Lewis that we would say our goodbyes there and then.

'No,' he said, 'I want to be with you until we say goodbye at Southampton.'

However, I feared that there might be questions asked regarding Pearl's age, and since I didn't want Mr. Lewis to be involved in any way, I planned accordingly. I had my hand luggage and my papers and passports all ready, and with my children at my side, I slipped into the crowd of people all waiting at the barrier to disembark. When my turn came, I saw that we had to go in single file through a narrow passageway between two

21

tables. My two little ones went in front of me, and I put my passport on the table to the left and my embarkation papers and so forth on the right hand table, saying to the officer in charge, 'Myself and two children, boy and girl.' My passport was stamped, my papers returned to me, and as we went through the barrier, I gave God a silent "thanks" for His blessing and our safe voyage.

Just then, while we were still on the ship, I heard my mother's voice saying, 'Here I am, Ritty, over here.' I had purposely avoided Mr. Lewis that morning, in case there was any embarrassment, and now, with seven hundred people disembarking, we missed each other in the crowd.

(We had had another farewell when we breakfasted that morning. Our fellow diner, who had been so difficult when we first came on board, had remained a silent partner at meal-times throughout the voyage. Now he held out his hand to me, I took it, and we wished each other goodbye. He said, 'I congratulate you, Mrs. Webb, on two wonderful children. To sit at your table has been a great pleasure, and your little ones are the best mannered and most well behaved children I have ever met.'

We parted the best of friends, and he even said that he hoped we would meet again some day.)

My mother took us to the railway station, and we set off for Somerset. As the train went through the beautiful countryside, I couldn't take my eyes off the scenery, it was so luscious and green. By now it was the beginning of August, and England was enjoying a heatwave, but the "green, green grass of home" seemed very cold to me after the straw-like grass and dried-up plains of Australia. The children snuggled up into the warm coats that I had made for them, also feeling the cold chill after the intense heat they had left. My own coat was a lined dust coat of black satin that I had taken out to Australia with me, and I was wearing it for the first time in six years. It had been too warm to wear, even in the Australian winter, but now, in this English summer heatwave it was not warm enough. My mother could see that we were very cold, and she said to me, 'It won't be long now, we'll soon be home, and I've told Dai to keep a big fire going for you.'

At last we reached the little village of Henstridge. We walked down a narrow winding lane, and on the left hand side stood the prettiest little cottage I think I have ever seen, surrounded by its own garden. This was my mother's home. She said that after I had left for Australia she and my step-father, Dai, had found themselves so alone that they had sold up their Welsh home and come to Somerset to live, near my brother Ben and his wife Maud, and their five children (two of whom had been born in my mother's house in Ogmore Vale). My mother loved Maud very much, and thought more of her and was more at home with her than with her own children, but, as she told me, Henstridge was convenient for London, and she could always slip up and stay with my sister Violet and her husband Fred if she ever felt like a break. Violet and Fred had two lovely children, Patricia and John.

'And then,' Mam said, 'I can go on to Mitcham and stay with your brother Garfield and his wife, and their little boy John. But it is here in Somerset that I want to live, where I can be near to Ben and Maud and their little girls.'

To Ben's little girls my mother was their very special "Granny Moggo" (Granny Ogmore).

Somerset was indeed a very beautiful place to come home to, and that night, when I climbed the stairs to the room where my children and I shared a double bed, I closed the bedroom door and looked at the stout solid walls, and felt their safety and my freedom from the fear that had been my portion for the last six years. Then all those old horrors and fears came back to me, the hardship and the anxieties that I had suppressed, and they crowded in on me and crushed me. I cannot describe the feeling that I had at that moment, but I just went to pieces in the quietness of that room, and cried and cried silently, not knowing why I was crying. All my pent-up emotions seemed to flood out of me in one terrible burst of crying.

My mother kept a big fire going all through the heatwave though she and my step-father couldn't bear the heat, but I still felt terribly cold. I wrote to Violet and asked her if she had a coat she could give me; she immediately sent me a pink mottled coat. My mother and I spent many days walking down the lovely winding lanes and enjoying the beautiful scenery, and I saw that I was a source of curiosity to the people we passed. I wondered why they stared at me, until I realised that while they walked along in skimpy tops and shorts, with the melting tar sticking to their shoes, I was wrapped up in a winter coat.

FOUR

After a week or two resting in the peace and quiet of the country, I took the children down to South Wales. I wanted to attend to some of my husband's business, so we went to stay with my sister-in-law, Dolly Mannings, in Humphries Terrace. We had arranged for all the family to meet at my late father-in-law's house in Maesteg on the following day, to discuss his will. He had been dead for several years, but his estate was still in the hands of his solicitor who told me that the children were unable to agree on the share-out of the property. The delay in settling the estate was also because the legal forms which had been sent to all the family for their signatures had had so far to go, (one had been sent to Ginny in the U.S.A., then to Canada for another daughter to sign, and then to Western Australia for Ivor's signature), that they had taken a whole year to complete.

Ivor's father had owned a substantial property, and the family at home had not been able to agree to any suggestions about its disposal; I was at the meeting to represent my husband. However they had also waited for my return because, so they said, my father had been a barrister, and so I would have a better knowledge of the law than they had. At that I told them I knew no more about it than they did, and we must use our common sense, because unless we settled matters as amicably and as soon as possible, there would be nothing left to fight over. Solicitors' fees alone could devour all the money realised by the sale of the property.

On their behalf I made an appointment to see a solicitor and put before him a proposition of my own which he thought was an excellent idea. All the property would be named and numbered separately; papers with the names and numbers of the properties, one for each parcel, would be put in one hat, and the names of each of Mr. Webb's nine children into another. Then, as the rest of the family refused to come to the office in person, the solicitor's clerk would take the name of a child from one hat, and the details

24

of a piece of property from another, and that property would go to that child. All the belongings not included in this arrangement had been assigned to the various children before my father-in-law's death, and were to be handed over after he died.

Some of the property drawn from the hat, like the business premises in Tonna Road which now became the property of my husband, Ivor, was of more value than the rest, and this had to be balanced. In our case we had to agree to pay one hundred and thirty pounds back into the estate, and similar arrangements were made for others, so that the bequests could be equalized, I didn't have one hundred and thirty pounds in cash, and Tom, Ivor's brother, didn't have the two hundred pounds he needed, so I made a further suggestion to the family that the three hundred and thirty pounds owed between us should be covered as a loan by the other members, so that the solicitor could settle up the affairs and release the deeds without incurring more expense. In a matter of weeks the whole affair was settled to everyone's satisfaction, and I was able to collect ten and sixpence a week rent from one of Ivor's properties. Now I would have a little more money coming in each week to keep myself and my children until Ivor came home.

(All the surplus money in the bank—quite a large sum—together with Farnham House and all its contents—was to be left to Desmond, Mr. Webb's fatherless grandson, to give him a home and provide for his education as a doctor.)

My husband's brother Will gave me a large envelope and told me to read it when I got home. 'Study it well,' he said, 'it concerns the business premises in Tonna Road which are now yours and Ivor's.' The envelope contained a copy of the lease of those premises, then occupied by the Co-operative Wholesale Society (CWS) on a six-year lease. Will told me that the Co-operative now wished to purchase the property and had given their offer to the solicitor, but the price they suggested was a hundred pounds more than the price the solicitor had quoted to me.

The property was structurally in excellent condition, having only been built a matter of twenty years previously, but the Co-op had sublet the living accommodation to two families, one on the top floor and one at the basement level, and both families had badly neglected the premises. They were now in a very dirty condition, but the business itself, which was on the ground floor, had been sealed off from the rest of the building. Conditions had been laid down in the lease to the effect that no part of the property was to be sublet at any time during the six years without the consent of the owner; if the owner did give permission to sublet, the Co-op were to pay the landlord a third of all the rent money collected from the sub-tenants. As no such permission had at any time been given, and as the solicitor who was conducting my father-in-law's business was also acting for the Co-operative, I went down to see him, to discuss the matter.

The solicitor said that he had thought that as we were in such dire need of money, we would be prepared to sell at any price, and insisted that the figure he had given us was the correct price. I pointed out to him that if I sold the property now, I would be depriving my huband of one and a half year's rental, together with the hundred and thirty pounds paid in to equalize the valuation of the property.

'You'll find that not only will there be no money for my husband, but he'll be in debt for vendor's fees from the sale of the property. I shall withdraw the sale until my husband returns from Australia,' I told him.

Then I went on to tell him of the conditions laid down in the lease concerning sub-tenants. At that the solicitor asked me how I knew all this; he had never seen the lease, and had not heard of any such conditions being laid down, so how could I have heard about it? I showed him a copy of the lease (having studied it well before going down to see him) and told him that I was now claiming all the moneys collected from the sub-tenants and owing to my husband from the past four years. A cheque was duly sent to me: not a fortune, but a much-needed amount of money which left me able to repay my sister-in-law the twenty-five pounds she had sent out to us in Australia.

I was also able to buy warmer clothes and more suitable shoes for my children and myself. Meanwhile, Mr. and Mrs. Mannings, my very kind sister-in-law and her husband, had been refusing to accept any money for our keep although they had four little ones of their own and my brother-in-law was out of work. Now I told them that I had been fortunate enough to find two rooms lower down the street, and I wanted to make a little home for the children and for Ivor when he got back. (I was hoping to be able to send for Ivor very soon, as his unmarried brother had promised to pay Ivor's fare home as soon as he received his money from the solicitor.) My brother-in-law shook me gently by the shoulders,

26

Christmas Day , 1932. Making our own fun in Western Australia
(beauty contest). Ivor Webb from Caerau and Dick Raymond
from Barry Island.

Little Pearl playing shy with the water
sellers in Columbo.

Jack in Columbo playing with ballo

Helen and I fishing in the Fitzroy River. There are crocs in this too, but we had a bathe in

and said to me, 'You're not taking these two children down their to starve, you're staying here.'

'We won't starve, Ted, the rent is only a small amount—just six shillings (30p) a week, and I'll be receiving ten and sixpence (52½p) a week from the rents of Bryn Glas. I've still got a little over ten pounds from the Co-operative money, which I put away for emergencies, like travelling costs if I have to go to Somerset. And anyway I've imposed on you and Dolly long enough. She has four children of her own to look after, without having me and my two pushed on to her. I am very grateful to you both for all you've done for me and my children.'

And so we took up residence with Mr. and Mrs. Cliff Orders, where our two rooms were very private and immaculate. They were a lovely family to live with, and their four children were always spotless.

The ten and sixpence was to be my weekly allowance to live on. Six shillings a week went for rent, which left me with four and sixpence; then sixpence a week went for paraffin oil for my lamp (I couldn't afford to use the electric). If I took a large bucket over to the coal yard, they would fill it with coal for sixpence, and with careful handling and my long training in hardship and economy out in Australia, we managed quite well.

I had bought Jack a pair of steel-cut shoes (which had small pieces of steel clipped into their soles to make them longer-lasting), and every night when I undressed him, I would examine his shoes to see if any of his steel clips had worked loose. If I saw any sign of the children's shoes wearing down, I would get out the foot last and "tap" (repair) them. I was a source of wonder to Mr and Mrs Orders, and many times caused them to laugh as they related that I was both shoe mender and barber to my children; I would laugh with them, and say, 'I'm Jack of all trades and master of none!'

Now I had to take my children to be registered with the local doctor, as I had to make sure they were in perfect health to meet the oncoming winter. I decided I would take them to Dr. Sinclair in Maesteg for a check-up. He examined the children, and said they were in perfect condition. 'But I am very concerned about you,' he said. I told him that I had been living in the bush in Australia, but I did not tell him my reasons for coming home. None the less, he took my hands in his and said, 'Do you know, you are a very, very lucky girl, coming back to this country.'

27

I didn't quite understand what he meant by this, but I said, but I said, 'Yes, I am lucky to be back.'

Looking earnestly into my face, he repeated, 'Very, very lucky.' Then he told me that I was suffering from suppressed fear, and said, 'Will you ask your husband to come and see me, I would like to talk to him.'

At that I told him that my husband was still in Australia. 'We didn't have enough money to come back together,' I explained.

He looked at me in astonishment and said, 'You can't mean to tell me you brought the children all this way by yourself.'

'I took them out when they were babies,' I said. 'It was much easier bringing them back.'

Then he asked me how many miles I had travelled back with them.

'Six hundred miles by land and fourteen thousand by boat, not counting the miles this side of the water,' I told him.

'When do you expect your husband to join you back here?' he asked.

I told him who my later father-in-law had been and explained that my husband's brother had promised to lend me the money for Ivor's fare as soon as he received his share from the solicitor. However, the doctor insisted, 'My dear, I need to see your husband as soon as possible, so that he can take some of the responsibility from you; you've had too much of it, and it's bad for you in your state of health.'

I didn't feel ill, and I couldn't understand his concern; he wasn't telling me anything I didn't already know. But the doctor's anxiety over my health was such that, quite unknown to me or any other member of the family, he visited our solicitor, and the two of them sent an urgent message out to Australia, telling Ivor to come home at once. He was to travel on the S.S. Hobsons Bay, which would bring him home in three months, and all expenses would be paid. However I was still unaware of the doctor's intervention in helping to get Ivor home, by the time that the next of our wanderings occurred.

FIVE

One day I received a telegram from my mother in Somerset, saying "Come back at once, I need you." I feared that something bad had happened, and I showed the telegram to Mr. and Mrs. Orders. I was sorry to leave them, but I promised that I would come back and take up my rooms again later, if they would have me. Then we hastened back to Somerset.

This was all excitement for the children, but it was just more worry for me, fearing my mother or stepfather was ill. Yet when I arrived at my mother's house, I found them both in the best of health! I believe that my mother thought I would be coming back a wealthy woman, though in fact I only had ten pounds in all the world. Naturally I asked my mother why she had sent for me to come at once. 'I have been alarmed,' I said, 'thinking that perhaps there was something wrong.'

'Oh no, Rit,' said my mother. 'I sent for you to come home because we have found the ideal place for you and Ivor to live. It's a farm, and you'll love it when you see it, Rit. We'll go and look at it.'

'Mam,' I said, 'I couldn't afford to buy a farm, I only have ten pounds, and I shall be giving that to you to keep the children and me.'

Still, to please my mother, we set off to see this beautiful farm, and walked along the narrow winding lanes for a mile or two, then left the lanes and went down through the fields. My mother said that there used to be a path through the fields, but it was overgrown now, as the place had been empty for a while. At last we came to a fairly large, but elderly building.

'This is it, Rit,' said my mother. She so excited. 'It's big enough for us all to live in. It will be lovely, Rit. You and Ivor can have one part of it, and Dai and I will have the other part. There's only one thing I don't like about it, and that's the old cellar underneath, but Ivor can board that up when he comes home.'

I tried to reason with my mother, and explain to her that it would take a fortune to restore the place, which had once, centuries ago, been an old wayside inn.

'Oh, we'll work on it,' she said. 'We'll soon put it right, the four of us together.

'It's a very lonely place to live in,' I told her. 'Just look at it, there isn't another house for miles around. When Ivor comes, he'll have to look for work—we can't live without money—and think of the children going to school in winter, they would have miles to walk.'

'Don't dampen my spirits now, Rit,' said my mother. 'I would love to come here to live.'

But I knew my mother and my stepfather better than they knew themselves. My stepfather was frightened of his own shadow, and would be no good living in a place like that, while mother was too much of a roamer to settle anywhere for long. However once she had set her mind on something, it was difficult to turn her away from it, and she had set her heart on this rundown old building, even though the country there was very flat, and with heavy rains was likely to be under water.

Something caught my eye at the side of the dilapidated old building. Mother said that it was the remains of a gibbet, and told me the story that she had heard from some old inhabitants of the village. 'Many years ago a road that was used by the mail coach went past here. There were one or two cottages dotted around too, so the little inn was where the farmers came in the evening for a drink and a chat. Now the place is referred to as "Jack White's Gibbet".'

We looked round, but there was no sign of the road or the cottages from where we were standing. My stepfather hadn't said anything all this time; he was afraid of going there to live, but he dared not say a word against it. I asked my mother if she could tell me more of the history of the place, and she continued.

'Far up in the fields was a cottage. A farm labourer lived in it, with his wife and their two boys, but when the boys grew up, one of them emigrated to Australia while the other stayed at home, labouring on the farm. The old couple did not hear from the son in Australia for several years, but one night the young man arrived home unexpectly. When they told him that his brother was down in the pub having a drink, he said he would go and surprise him there, and off he went. But before telling anyone who he was, he opened his wallet and ordered drinks all round. The

30

two brothers failed to recognise each other, and after flashing his money around a little too often, the Australian son decided to go home and wait for his brother there. On his way home he was robbed and murdered.

'When the other son got home, his mother asked him what he thought of Jack, who had surprised them by coming home from Australia and the lad realised that the man he had robbed and killed was his own brother. He was put in an iron cage, and hung from a gibbet to starve to death. No-one was allowed to give him food or drink under threat of being put in a cage themselves for aiding a prisoner. It was said that his mother had once put a candle through a little hole in the cage, but he was left there to rot.'

After that we went home, determined never to mention the place again. However, my mother brought the subject up once more, saying, 'Well, you've got plenty of money now.' I had to tell her that the money was Ivor's and I wouldn't touch a penny of it until he came home.

'I gave you all the money I had when I returned from Australia,' I said. 'I have arranged with Tom to send on to me the two pounds a month rent money, and you will have that regularly. I can't do anything more until Ivor comes home.'

My mother had been very spoilt, and was used to getting her own way in everything, so to show her displeasure with me, she said to the children, 'Come on, we'll go and pick blackberries.'

'How long will you be gone?' asked my stepfather.

'Oh, just long enough to make sufficient to make a tart.'

She said nothing to me. I did all the household chores, but my mother did the cooking, and if I spoke to her, she wouldn't answer me, but just give a grunt and ignore me. When they had been gone for several hours, I began to be worried about the children, who had had no dinner, and my stepfather started parading up and down the garden path, looking over the gate. Then he would come back into the house and say, 'No sign of them yet, Rit.'

'How long would it take them to get to the blackberries, Dai?' I asked him.

'Well,' he said, 'there are blackberries all around here, it wouldn't take her ten minutes to pick enough for a tart.'

I suggested that I should go to look for them, but Dai said, 'No, Rit, you'd get lost, then we would have to come looking for you, because there are dozens of little lanes around here, and we don't know which one she's taken.'

31

My stepfather seemed very worried and agitated, and he added, 'All I hope is that she hasn't gone into one of the fields, looking for the bigger, sweeter blackberries.'

'Well, wouldn't the farmer let them go into the field, then?' I asked him.

'Oh yes,' he said, 'but there is a bloody big bull in the field.'

I trembled so much at hearing the word "bull" that I had to sit down, and I remembered what had happened in the Northampton show in Western Australia. I left the same fear over again as we did then, when the bull broke loose and pounded towards us as we stood by the sheep pens, my sister Emily and I, and the six children; we had watched in horror as he tossed horse and rider into the air, and we saw them fall again, the horse badly slashed along its side. Now this fear gripped me once more, and I could picture my mother and my children being tossed by this English bull. I covered my face with my hands, and cried, and thought, "Have I brought my children through all our hardships and fears, and through that long voyage, only for them to be killed by a bull."

They had been gone for four hours now, although my mother had said she would be back in ten minutes when they left. I stood at the gate with my stepfather, hoping and praying that God would bring them back safely to me. Then I heard the happy chatter of my children as they came down the lane. I ran to meet them, hugging them and crying, which annoyed my mother. But she had no idea of the dangers and the fears that I had experienced over the last six years, or the fact that my health had broken and I had been ordered home by the doctors. I had told her nothing about his, so I couldn't really blame her for the way in which she flew into a rage or the unkind things she said to me. It all stemmed from the disappointment she had had when I refused to buy or to live in "Jack White's Gibbet". She told my stepfather she had taken the children visiting, and that was why she had been away for so long. I couldn't really defend myself against my mother, because I had never in my life had a cross word with her, and when she remained silent for days refusing to speak to me, it made me very unhappy.

I had started Jack and Pearl in the little village school, and they were happy there. It was a very pretty place, and I would have been quite content to make my home there and wait for Ivor to come back. (I was receiving Ivor's letter every week, but each letter was seven weeks old by the time it reached me, and I waited with every one for news of his homecoming.)

One morning I took my two little ones for a walk, just to get out of the unfriendly atmosphere at my mother's home. The two months' rent was due that day, but it hadn't arrived, and I had the feeling that my mother had now tired of us. She hadn't said so, but I sensed we had outstayed our welcome. As we walked along, the air felt so clean, the scenery was beautiful, and everything looked fresh and bright. I was busy telling the children how pleased Daddy would be when he saw what a lovely place we were now living in. There was no mechanized traffic on the road, so the children could romp about, and we would stop to admire the cottages, all ablaze with flowers at the front and with neat kitchen gardens at the back. It was such a serene and peaceful life, all I could wish for, and an ideal place to bring up my children.

We passed a row of little thatched cottages, and I noticed that the end cottage was empty. A woman from the house next door came out and asked me if I was thinking of renting the empty cottage.

'It's only one room up and one down, and the rent is one and sixpence ($7\frac{1}{2}$p) a week,' she told me.

I did some quick mental arithmetic, and my heart leapt with joy. 'Yes, we'll go there to live,' I said immediately. It didn't matter to me that we had no furniture—as long as we were surrounded by four solid walls, that was all that mattered to me. We would be left with eight and sixpence ($42\frac{1}{2}$p) a week, after rent, to live on, and we could manage all right until Ivor came home. The children were delighted at the prospect of going there to live, but I didn't know how I was going to approach the subject with my mother. To my surprise, however, when I got back a letter had arrived in the second post with the two pounds rent money. My mother was a changed woman when I put the two pounds in her hand; she said, 'I'm glad you're back, Rit. Dai and I were just getting ready to go out shopping.' So the two pounds had given me a new lease of life for at least another month.

I told my mother about the cottage, and asked her if she would lend me the bed we were sleeping in, and the little table and two kitchen chairs that were in the wash house.

My mother said, 'You can't go there to live, you are all right here.' But I knew that if the money didn't arrive on time the following month, I'd be back in the doghouse again, and I longed

33

to live in the little cottage. There were no mod. cons. there and no electricity, but to me it was heaven! I told my mother I could use the oil lamp for lighting, and there was plenty of wood in the coppice close by, so I wouldn't have to buy coal, and I would have a home of our own to welcome Ivor to when he came home. However my mother wouldn't hear of it. 'Ivor can come here,' she said.

She had rented a wireless on hire purchase, the first one we had ever seen; but since we didn't know anything about volume, we could only get a faint sound from it. So we put it in the middle of the table, and then we would all sit around it, our heads almost touching the case, to try and hear the broadcasts. We thought it was wonderful!

One day I was talking to a cottager, and she told me that all the women did "gloving" in their homes. She said to me, 'Come in tonight, my dear, and some of my neighbours will come in and we'll sit around, then I will teach you how it is done.'

After a few evenings of watching the women at work, I asked her how I would be able to get some of this work to do in my mother's cottage. 'Well, my dear,' she said, 'You'll have to go to the factory, 'tis only a little place in a village eight miles away. You'll have to walk it, my dear, and walk back again, 'tis the only way you'll get to he, and tell he, my dear, I've shown you the work and will he send work up to 'ee next Saturday.'

The next morning, early, I set off to walk the eight miles to the factory. When I arrived, I asked the young man if he could give me some gloving to do, and on hearing my Welsh accent, he wanted to know where I had come from.

'How did you get here?' he asked.

'I walked,' I told him.

'Good gracious,' he said. 'How are you going to get back?'

'The same way as I came,' I replied.

'Well, you shall certainly have work to do,' he said. 'We'll collect your work on Saturday, and give you a new batch to do, together with your wages.'

The work was duly delivered to me. I got up early and cleaned the cottage—it wasn't large, and was quite easy to keep clean. The cold weather was now creeping in, and it was nice to sit by a log fire after all the housework was done, and work at my gloving. My job was to put fleecy linings inside kid gloves, and the only tool for the job was a broom-like handle which stood on a base on the

34

floor. I would sit with the base between my legs and the handle at a comfortable height to work on; the top of the handle was pointed, to fit into the finger of the glove. It was skilled work, and great care was needed in turning the fingers and stitching the lining to the inside of the finger. When I became expect at that job, I was put onto hand sewing kid gloves with leather thongs and sharp crewel needles. I made quite a nice sum of money each week, so we could live comfortably, and my mother was more amiable now that there was money coming into the house.

SIX

At last news came that Ivor was embarking on the Hobsons Bay, and would be home in seven weeks' time. When the great day dawned, we hired a car and went to Southampton to meet him; it was the 24th of October, a very wet and cold day when he arrived. (When we were coming back from Southampton, the fields were under water and looked like miniature lakes!)

Ivor had had a pleasant voyage, with no responsibilities and money in his pocket, all of which was the work of the solicitor and Dr. Sinclair. It was lovely to have him home, and know that at last we were a family again.

Since Ivor was now able to put his defence bonds in at the Post Office and get cash repayment, he could go shopping for more suitable clothes, including a warm, heavy overcoat. He said we would have to go back to Wales, because he had a lot of business to attend to; and he wanted to see the man whom he had left in charge of his colliery contract, and find out from him why I had only been given four pounds, ten shillings (£4.50) and allowed to suffer such hardships, when he should have given me three hundred pounds, which would have left me comfortably off. I left it to Ivor to break it to my mother that he was taking me and the children back to Wales; we were busy packing up our clothes, ready for the train journey back to Careau.

'You can't leave us here, Ivor,' said my mother. 'We are not stopping here on our own, we are coming with you.'

I told her that we had nowhere to take her to; I didn't even know where we would be staying ourselves. And my mother had no money, her old age pension was only one pound a week, with a pound for my stepfather. On the morning we were leaving, I tried to reason with my mother, but she was adamant, 'You are not leaving me behind,' she kept saying, and before daybreak a van arrived at the cottage. Ivor told her that he had only enough money to get us back to Wales, and we didn't know where we were going to live, or with whom, but my mother and Dai were already

36

packing their furniture into the van. Ivor tried to reason with her once more, saying he had only just enough money to pay for our fares, and he could not pay for a van, but she just said, 'Don't worry, just get the things in, and we'll get up on top.'

So my mother and Dai rode with the driver, and Ivor and I and the children had to struggle and make do in the back of the van, lying on top of all the furniture, bits of sticks and so forth. The only cover on that long, uncomfortable journey from Somerset down to Wales was a tarpaulin, which kept us warm and prevented the furniture from falling off the open van. We left Somerset at eight o'clock in the morning, and arrived in Caerau at eight o'clock that night.

'Take us down to Hermon Road,' my mother said. 'I know someone there who will take us in—Bob and Lydia Bowen.'

'Are you sure they are still living there?' I asked. 'It must be years since you saw them last.'

'Well, we will go there, and try. I don't know anyone else,' my mother answered.

When we arrived at Bob and Lydia's house, it was empty; they had gone away to live, and the neighbours didn't know where they were. We didn't know what to do, and Ivor said, 'Well, we'll have to take all the stuff up to Protheroe Street, and put it in Father's shed.'

So off we went, higher up the valley, to Protheroe Street. Ivor and I were lying on top of the furniture, underneath the tarpaulin, but we made the children comfortable lower down in the van. We could not see where we were going, because the tarpaulin was covering us, but to get to Protheroe Street we had to go under the railway bridge, where the headroom was low. The driver did not realise that the bridge was too low for the height of his load, and he went on towards it; then he suddenly saw a man at the side of the road, waving his hands frantically and shouting, 'Stop, for God's sake, or you'll be crushed to death!'

The driver pulled up dead and we peeped out from under the tarpaulin; we were almost touching the roof of the bridge. Ivor was as white as a sheet, and so was the driver. Thanks to the promptness of the man in waving to the driver, we had been saved from being crushed to death as we lay on top of the furniture.

Ivor was annoyed that we had been put to all this trouble at a time when we could well have done without it. Now he was not

37

only responsible for his own wife and family, but also for his mother- and father-in-law and all their furniture.

'Now what do we do?' said Ivor.

There was nothing for it but to back the van into the side of the road. The only way up to Protheroe Street was under the bridge, and the loaded van was too high to go through it.

'Well,' said Ivor, after a moment's thought, 'there's nothing else for it, we'll have to go back down the valley; Father had a shed there, on the black tips.'

Down we went, through Gelli Street, the big van rumbling along, and drawing many people out to their front doors to see what was roaring through their street at that time of night. It was early November, cold and dark. We got down off the van because it had to go under another low bridge, and a woman shouted to us, 'Where do you think you are going with that load at this time of night?' I was too cold and stiff, after that painful journey, to bother to answer her, but my mother told her that we had come down from Somerset; she said that the house where we had been going to stay was empty and the people had gone away, and now we were going to try to put the furniture in Mr. Webb's shed, on the other side of the line.

The woman looked spotlessly clean, and her home looked warm and inviting. My mother asked her, 'Do you know of anyone who has two rooms to let, for my husband and me? My daughter and her family have her husband's people to go to, but the furniture is mine and my husband's.'

The woman told my mother that she wouldn't be able to take the van under the bridge because it was too low. 'But I've got two rooms,' she said, 'if you would like to come here.'

The driver of the van and Ivor and the man of the house soon got the furniture into the house, and in a short time, while the men were putting the bed up, my mother got a nice fire going, and made a pot of tea for herself and Dai. I thought that she would ask us to stay the night then, as we were so cold, but all she said was, 'Oh, thank goodness for that, now Dai and me can have some supper and get straight to bed.' There was no thought of me or the children, sitting outside in the van, freezing cold. She obviously thought we would be taken care of, but now we had to walk about a mile, in the bitter cold, to find someone who would take us in.

Ivor's sister Dolly was sharing her house with her brother and his wife and their two children, so though she could put up Ivor and Jack in the same room as her own boys, she had no room for Pearl and me. We had to walk up to Ivor's old family home in Protheroe Street, and Ivor asked me if we would be alright on the long journey. Two of Ivor's sisters lived there now, but when I got there, the house was in darkness. They had all gone to bed.

I rang the bell, and the door was opened by Ivor's youngest sister, who was now married and had a little boy of her own. She told me that the other sister, Gertie, had also married and gone to live in Swansea with her husband and little boy, and she was renting the house from them. She took us into the kitchen, and said, 'Goodnight, Ray, I'm going back to bed now.' The fire had gone out but the room was still a little warm, so Pearl and I lay down on the wooden settle and curled up together, and I spread my coat over us. We still felt cold, but with the coat around us, and holding each other close, we were able to maintain our body heat.

At half past five the following morning, we were wakened by Ivor's youngest unmarried brother, Albert, who was getting himself off to work. When he saw Pearl and me lying on the wooden settle, with my coat as our blanket, he said, 'Have you two been sleeping there all night?' Albert made us a hot drink and gave us something to eat before he went to work, and as he was going out, he said, 'Don't worry, Ray, you'll have a warm bed to sleep in tonight, you won't be sleeping on that thing.'

As soon as it was daylight, I took my little girl and went down to Humphries Terrace, to Ivor. When I knocked at Dolly's door, she was preparing her little boys for school, but there was always a welcome from Dolly, and although I knew she had no room for us to stay at night, we would be able to enjoy the warmth of her home in the daytime. We would just have to make do at night.

Ivor's eldest brother, Will, his wife, Elizabeth Anne, and their two boys lived in the front part of the house, and Dolly and her family lived at the back. I didn't tell them of the haphazard reception we had received in Protheroe Street, though I think they realised. However Will and his wife were annoyed because they had not known of our predicament until a chance remark from Ivor the night before had told them I had gone up to sleep in Winnie's. Will said, 'Ray, Elizabeth Anne and I talked it over last night, and we've decided that you and Ivor and the children are to stay here in our place, and we will go and stay further along the street with Elizabeth's parents. You are welcome to stay here as long as you like, we'll be quite happy down with Mammy and Daddy.'

We were very happy there for several weeks. It was beautifully furnished and spotlessly clean. Will didn't work; he had been all through the 1914-18 war and had come back without a scratch—only to go back to the colliery and break his spine in an accident. We were very grateful for their kindness towards us, but I felt guilty that we were keeping them out of their house—with Christmas only a fortnight away, I couldn't bear the thought of depriving their children of their own room. So I looked around for two rooms, and was lucky enough to find them with nice people in Hermon Road. I went to see my mother, to ask her if she would give me some of her spare furniture, and she gave me a double bed, some warm bedclothes, and an iron-framed bedchair big enough for the two children, with bedclothes to keep them warm too. Then we moved out, and were able to tell Will and Elizabeth Anne to return to their own home. They stressed that they were in no hurry to return, but I told them, 'I love you for your kindness to us, and I can't impose on that kindness any longer.'

SEVEN

We were still only having the ten shillings a week rent from the one house; the rent from the other property was paid every four months, and was not due yet. I made two loaves of Christmas cake, and gave one of them to my mother, then I went to the market to see what I could buy for the children's Christmas presents. I bought a nice, dressed doll for a few shillings for Pearl, and for Jack, a very colourful cardboard farmhouse which had to be fixed into position, and some boxes of farm animals which cost just a few coppers. As it was Christmas Eve, the market was selling off some large annuals very cheaply, so I bought one each for the children; they were a shilling each.

All I had left after buying the toys was one shilling, and I still had to get my poultry. Ivor and I went to the butcher's to see what I could buy; I wasn't worried that I only had a shilling left to spend, because I knew I would be able to buy a big piece of belly pork for that money (5p). When I was ordering it, Ivor said to the butcher, 'Put another shillingsworth on.' Belly pork had gone up to sixpence a pound, so I would only have been able to buy two pounds for my shilling. My children had never seen a real butcher's shop in their lives, so although we were only buying two shillingsworth of belly pork, it was a great thrill for us to stand in the shop and look around at all the poultry hanging up, and the legs of pork for those who could afford them. We didn't feel a twinge of envy for the people who *could* afford these things, and we went home quite happy, and prepared for Christmas.

On Christmas morning there were no two children in the world happier than my two, with the gifts that Father Christmas had given them, and seeing *them* so happy made Ivor and me happy too. Although we only had a scrubbed table and a few kitchen chairs in the one and only living room, the four of us were together. We would shut our door and enjoy the warmth of our own fire, and I wouldn't have changed places with anyone in the world. I felt like a queen, and my husband was king of his castle,

41

because although we had no fine house, and not a penny to our name, we had the most precious gift of all—"love at home".

On Boxing Day, towards dinner time, Ivor answered a knock at the door. Two men stood on our doorstep, and Ivor recognised them both. One was the manager of Caerau Colliery, where Ivor had worked as a contractor before going to Australia, and the other was a school mate of his who was now the manager of Waun Tarw Colliery near Llanharan. They had both arrived at our doorstep at the same time and with the same purpose in mind, to offer Ivor work. They had both heard that "Webb" was back in Caerau, and each had hoped to be the first one to offer him a job. Good contractors were hard to find.

An argument arose between the two managers, and they almost came to blows because Glyn Evans, the manager of Waun Tarw, said he had prior claim on Ivor, his old school pal, and the manager of Caerau, Mr. Pomeroy, said he had prior claim because the Webbs had always had the contract with them. Ivor didn't ask them in, and I didn't know if it was because our home was so poor, or because I had made Ivor promise me that he would never again go to work on the hard ground. The wages were great, but the risk to life was greater, and we had intended to make our home by the seaside, in Porthcawl, when Ivor's money came through. Ivor couldn't make up his mind. The work in Caerau would be nearer for him, and a contract would soon get us out of the poverty we were in.

Then Ivor thought of his brother Tom, who had been kind enough to look after Ivor's property, and had regularly sent the rent to me while I was in Somerset. He had been a fireman in Caerau Colliery. Firemen are officials whose duty it is to see to shotfiring into the coal headings, breaking up the coal so that the colliers can get at it, and it is a very responsible job, because they have to make sure that the powder (which is called "firedamp") is quite dry before firing. Many firemen took the firedamp home with them after their shift and put it into the oven to dry. Tom would not subject his wife and children to the danger of doing this, although it was of benefit to the shot firer to have the powder dried at home. (It was also against the law to do this, as the powder was gunpowder.)

On one particular day, Tom's shot had misfired, and although no-one had been hurt, the accident could have caused an explosion and injury to many men. The rule of the colliery was that any fireman who misfired his shot would be instantly dismissed, and though Tom was a very good and conscientious fireman, the rules could not be waived for one man. So he was dismissed, and had been out of work for a long time.

Ivor said to the managers, 'To save any argument, I will tell you that I would very much like to work at my old colliery, particularly as I have an old score to settle with a man I left in charge of my contract. I mean the man who should have given my wife three hundred pounds that would have kept her comfortably off while she was waiting to join me in Australia, but actually only gave her four pounds ten shillings (£4.50). I would very much like to meet up with him again. But on the other hand, Glyn, I would very much like to work with you, for old time's sake, so we'll best decide it this way. The first man to offer my brother Tom a job as fireman in his colliery will be the one I work for.'

Glyn quickly said, 'I will take him, Ivor, Tom was a good fireman, and deserves another chance.'

Mr. Pomeroy said, 'I'm sorry I can't give the same answer. I would willingly take Tom back, but the union would not allow it. And the man you want to see, Ivor, is no longer at Caerau Colliery. He was killed on the conveyor belt a few days ago.'

So Tom and Ivor started work, and Tom found lodgings in Pencoed. Glyn told Ivor to bring me and the children down to stay with his family until we could find a suitable place, and Ivor took us down there. It was a beautiful big house, and we were made very welcome, but I wanted a place of our own, and Ivor soon found a nice house to rent in Brynna. Then Ivor went up to his father's shed on the black tips, and collected some furniture, including a large sideboard that had been in the dining room on King George's ship, which had some time previously been brought into dock to be dismantled. My father-in-law, before his death, had gone up to London Docks and bought all the furniture that had been on the ship. He had had a large shed built on the black tips of Caerau, and employed a cabinet maker to make the furniture suitable for ordinary houses. Much of it had been distributed amongst his children and this large sideboard had been given to Ivor. We also had a gentleman's hall wardrobe that had been in his majesty's room.

We had had these pieces of furniture before we left for Australia, as well as a beautiful mahogany bureau which had been of use in his majesty's stateroom. However, owing to the fact that

43

we had had only a few hours' notice that Ivor would be sailing for Australia and I would be going to live with my mother in Ogmore Vale, the large sideboard had been sent down to the shed to be stored, HM wardrobe had gone to Ivor's sister, and Nurse Aubrey had begged me to give her the bureau. I felt I owed her something for helping me with my baby when she was ill with pneumonia, and at that time I didn't realise the value of the furniture, so I let her take it. Now my sister-in-law gave the wardrobe back, and we had the sideboard. Ivor built me a bureau out of pieces of mahogany from the shed, so our home was building up.

We were very comfortable in our new house. The children started school in Brynna, but then Jack became very poorly, and had to attend a T.B. clinic. The doctor there said he was going to put him into Cefn Hirgoed Hospital, but I said to him, 'Tell me, doctor, is my son negative or positive?'

'At the moment,' he said, 'he's negative.'

'In that case,' I said, 'I will not allow my child to go into a tubercular hospital. I will nurse him at home.'

The doctor was adamant that the child had to go to hospital, but I was just as adamant that he should not. I said to the doctor, 'I bring this child to your clinic every fortnight. He's stripped and left to stand naked in this biting cold clinic until you are ready to see him, then I take him home, and for the next fortnight he's a sick child, due to being exposed to such intense cold here. You don't realise that this child has been reared in the intense heat of the tropics, and you want to give him the cold treatment he would receive in the T.B. hospital; if he is also subjected to living and breathing in the same ward as tubercular patients, then I'm afraid he would surely become "positive". No thank you, sir, this is the last time you will have the pleasure of seeing my child freezing in your clinic.'

I didn't take my child there again. However, I told my own doctor that although we liked living in Brynna, it was our intention to take the children to live by the sea, in Porthcawl, as soon as it was possible. He told me that the sea air around our coasts would be too strong for Jack, he wouldn't live three months in Porthcawl. 'The air in Brynna is also too strong for him,' he said. 'My advice to you is to take him further inland.'

One day, when I was shopping in Bridgend, I met Mrs. Owen, an old friend of mine from Ogmore Vale. She was making a fuss of my children, and said she had boys and girls who would love to meet them. She was living on the mountain in Bryncethin, she told me, and her husband was the head of the unemployment exchange in Bridgend. She invited us over for a visit.

There were six large, detached houses on the common, called Caehelig. It was a lovely place, ideal for bringing up children; the air was so clean and fresh, and they had all the mountain to play on.

'You must come up here to live,' said Lilian Owen. 'See how attached my children have become to yours. They would love it here. My neighbour John Jones's father, who was a crofter, built these six houses for his children, and his daughter lived in this one. She had an unhappy marriage, and died unexpectedly, so John rented it to Edward, my husband. John lives in that big house on his own—he married the post mistress, but she died five years later. I'll go down and ask John if he will let you some rooms. He's a very nice man. He's never let any of his rooms, but I'll have a talk with him.'

She came back after a little while, bringing John with her. He was a tall, good-looking gentleman of about sixty. He was rather unwilling to share his house, particularly with someone with two small children, so when Lilian introduced me to him, I said, 'I quite understand you not wanting to share your house with us. Such a lovely house you have—I would feel the same as you if I owned it, I wouldn't like the thought of children running around, especially as you had no children of your own.

John said at last, 'I have changed my mind, Mrs. Owen. I think what my house needs is the sound of children, and I will be happy to share my home with Mrs. Webb and her family.'

I asked Mrs. Owen if she had told him that there would soon be another child, and she said, "Yes, she had told him". So the following Saturday, Ivor, the children and I took up residence in Croft House, where we had four lovely large rooms and all the front of the house was ours. While we were living in Brynna, Ivor had bought himself a motorbike to travel to work and back; it was a powerful "Red Indian", so the extra miles he now had to travel to work didn't make any difference. My two little ones took an instant liking to John, as did my husband and myself; he was a real gentleman, and I couldn't have wished for a nicer home to live in.

EIGHT

One time when we lived in Australia, Ivor had given me two pounds. It had been the first money he had given me in years, because of the depression out there, and I was so surprised at receiving the two pounds that I had made a rash statement. 'If ever we go back to England,' I said, 'and I am given two pounds every week, I shall be very happy!' Now here we were, back in Wales, and Ivor had taken on a contract where his wages would be roughly eighty pounds a week. One day he took me into Bridgend, and spent quite a lot of money on us. He bought me an expensive coat and hat, with everything to match, and warm winter clothing for the children, and he bought himself an expensive motor bike. (He wouldn't buy anything on credit.) All this was to soften the blow that was to come!

Next Ivor said to me, 'Sit down, we have a lot to discuss.' I dutifully sat down, and wondered what was coming. 'You know we borrowed a hundred and twenty five pounds from my brother Will and my sister Dolly, to equalize the property in Caerau; then, when the solicitor booked my passage home on the "Hobson's Bay", he also sent me all my travel expenses and pocket money for the journey from Southampton to Somerset. That was an awful lot of money, and we also owe Dolly and Ted the twenty five pounds they sent out to us in Australia.'

I told him that we didn't owe the twenty five pounds to Dolly and Ted, because I had already settled that. Then Ivor said, 'You remember what you told me out in Australia, that if you had two pounds a week you would be happy? Well, I am going to hold you to that promise. Will you take two pounds a week until all our debts are cleared?'

I was flabbergasted. Things were different now, I had to try and build up a new home for us. I said, 'The old iron bed-chair was only a makeshift, and I wanted a new oak bed for the children. And I need to replace the old iron bed with the straw-filled mattress that we sleep on with a new modern bed and bedroom suite.'

46

I agreed with Ivor that all our debts had to be paid first, before we could ever begin to think of rebuilding our home, but although I knew Ivor did not like buying anything on credit, in a shop in Bridgend I had seen two beds which I could buy for five shillings a week. This would leave me with one pound fifteen shillings a week to keep four of us and pay the rent. I bought the two beds, but I knew that Ivor and I would have to wait for *our* new bed until I had finished paying for the others.

* * *

A little brook ran down from the top house, and on its opposite bank was a piece of marshland or bog. One day, as Ivor was coming home from work, he saw a crowd of people standing by the bog, and went to investigate. He saw a horse sinking into the bog, its hindquarters already sunk down into it, and he could see that the men who were trying to help the horse were shouting so much that they were causing it to panic and sink faster. Ivor said to them, 'Keep quiet, leave the horse alone, and someone get a plank and coil of rope.'

There were quickly brought to him, and he put the plank across the bog, as near to the horse as possible. Then he crawled across the plank and got the rope underneath the horse's legs and around his shoulders, knotted it, and threw the other end across to the waiting men, telling them to pull gently, while he stayed out in the bog, soothing and encouraging the frightened horse. Eventually they brought it to safety. Then the men told Ivor that the horse had been the first one to come out of that bog; many had gone in, but none had come out before.

We had only been living in Caehelig for a few weeks when Ivor went out one Saturday night for a quiet drink on his own, down at the Royal Oak. This was only a few yards from our house, at the side of the main Bridgend to Ogmore road. Bryncethin was a sleepy little hamlet, not an industrial area; it was farming country and the same families had lived there for generations. It was a peace-loving community, and most of the people conversed in Welsh. There was one particular house, standing in its own grounds, where a Mr. Bates and his unmarried nephew lived. Mr. Bates was an Englishman, and he and his nephew considered themselves a cut above everyone else; they ruled the village with a rod of iron. Practically the whole of the village lived in awe of the Bateses, I don't know why.

47

That Saturday night was very cold, and Ivor was sitting near the fire in the lounge of the Royal Oak. The man sitting next to him was a boxer, a coloured man who told Ivor he was the son of a negro father and a white mother. It was very peaceful inside the pub, but the peace was suddenly disturbed by the sound of blows from outside the window. Ivor asked the man sitting beside him what the noise was about, and he said, 'Oh, that's Bates's nephew, I expect, giving someone a punch up.'

Just then a man pushed open the door and said to the boxer, 'Come quick, Bates is beating up old John Jones, he's half killed him.'

The boxer said, 'No, I am not getting mixed up in anything to do with the Bateses,' but Ivor threw his coat off and was out of that pub in an instant when he heard the name John Jones. (He knew John Jones must be our landlord, and knew he was much too quiet to get involved in a fight, especially with the Bates family.) Ivor caught Bates by the scruff of the neck and gave him a blow which sent him staggering across the road. Next he picked John up, and after asking someone to take care of him, went back to Bates and gave him a leathering. Then he went back into the pub and sat down to finish his drink.

John Jones had gone into the pub to recover, and Ivor said to the boxer, 'You are not much of a cobber or you would have gone out there to help that old man.' But the boxer said, 'You wouldn't have gone if you knew Bates like we do. Anyone who offends Bates might as well pack up and leave the valley. You won't have work anywhere, and if you are already in a job, they'll soon get you out of it. No-one around here would employ you—and you are sitting in his seat, mate, not one of us would dare do that. If he comes in, you'll have to get up.'

'Has he bought this seat, then?' asked Ivor.

'No,' said the boxer.

'Well then, let him come in and make me get out, I'm not shifting for him.'

In the meantime, it appears that Bates had come into the pub, seen Ivor sitting on his seat, and gone out, determined to have his revenge on John Jones. John had left the public bar, intending to go home, but the other man was waiting for him outside. Bates was a big, powerfully built man, and John wasn't able to defend himself against the bully when he started to beat him up again.

Ivor was quickly out there, to find John in a very bad state; the

48

old man's brothers carried him across the road to their house, while Ivor gave Bates the finest thrashing he had ever had in his life. Meanwhile the doctor had been sent for to attend to John, and the publican had called the police. There were no police cars in those days, so they took longer to arrive on the scene, but the sergeant and two police officers soon turned up and said to Ivor, 'It's all right, we'll take him now.'

'No you won't,' said Ivor. 'Not until I have finished giving him what he gave John Jones!' But the policemen dragged Ivor away from Bates; then, with one of the officers on either side of him, Bates was led away.

The sergeant stopped to talk to Ivor, and said to him, 'Thank you, sir, we have been wanting to have something on this bugger for a long time, he has been terrorising this village for years, and the people are too frightened of him and his uncle to do anything about it.'

Bates was locked up that night, and on the following day his uncle went to see him, but couldn't recognise him because he was so badly beaten up. Bates told his uncle that the police had beaten him up.

One day in August I called to pick up my children from school, and as we came near our house, I noticed Ivor speaking to the sergeant of police. I had been told nothing of the fight that had taken place at the pub, and I was frightened at seeing the sergeant outside my house. Ivor explained to the sergeant that I knew nothing about the fight because my time was near and he didn't want me distressed. John was being cared for by his two sisters-in-law in the village, so I hadn't seen him, and I was unaware of the damage he had suffered, but it would have upset me greatly if I *had* known about it. The sergeant assured me there was nothing wrong.

'We were just having a friendly chat,' he said.

The sergeant had been telling Ivor that Mr. Bates was suing him and his two police officers for assaulting his nephew, and Bates was going to do everything in his power to strip the sergeant of his rank and drive his policemen from the force; he was asking Ivor if he would come to court in their defence. The sergeant promised that Ivor wouldn't be called unless things went against them.

'That man,' said the sergeant, 'has the power and the means to do what he wants, and you are our only hope, Mr. Webb, as you are the only one who can witness that he was in that state when we took him to gaol.'

The day of the trial came, and Ivor took a shift off to go to court. It was the beginning of October, 1933, and the case was being heard at the Bridgend Police Courts. Ivor was not in the court, but was just waiting in case he was called, though the sergeant had promised that he would only be asked to appear as a last resort. Bates had the best solicitor money could buy, and he was certain that he was going to get the three policemen. He insisted that all his injuries were inflicted on him in the police cell, and claimed that the two policemen had held him while the sergeant beat him up.

When everything seemed to be going against them, the sergeant asked if he could call his witness. Ivor was called in, and when he walked through the doorway of the courtroom, there was a gasp; he was six feet tall, and bronzed, and filled the door frame. He was sworn in and asked if he recognised anyone in the court. Ivor was a very refined and well-spoken man, and when he was asked the question, he pointed to Bates and said, 'Yes, that is the man I beat up.'

The judge said to Ivor, 'You admit that you beat that man up?'

'Yes, sir, I do,' replied Ivor.

'Why did you beat him up?' asked the judge.

'Because he beat up a defenceless old man who couldn't raise a hand to defend himself. I wanted that bully to feel for himself the pain he had inflicted on that helpless old man. I'm afraid I lost myself completely in my determination to make him suffer as he had made that old man suffer, and he can thank his lucky stars that the police intervened, because if they hadn't pulled him away from me, he would have been in his coffin.'

'You admit, then,' said the judge, 'that it was you and not the police who inflicted those injuries on Mr. Bates?'

'Yes, sir,' Ivor said, 'and as I have said, if the police hadn't arrived when they did, I would be standing here defending my life, because I would have killed him.'

The police were exonerated, and the case went against Bates. They hoisted my husband out and carried him into the York Hotel, where they had a big celebration. The headlines in the Gazette took up the whole front page: "POLICE VERSUS BATES". Bates and his uncle disappeared after the case, and no-one heard of them again. John didn't return home to Croft House until his face was completely healed.

NINE

My children found life very exciting after the quietness of the bush, and they enjoyed their new freedom from fear. (They couldn't understand why they could run so freely round the mountains and not meet any snakes or other poisonous creatures.) And life for them was doubly exciting because they had the Owen children to play with, and three little girls of Pearl's age. By now they had forgotten their usual game of "Gilly gilly", which they had learnt from children in Columbo, and in other parts that we had visited.

They had found life very dull in the Australian bush. Even our first Christmas in Australia was spent quietly; my mother had sent some presents for the children, including a carpenter's set for Jack, who was about three years old at the time, and he had a passion for rusty nails. He couldn't pass a nail without picking it up—"for Daddy", he used to say. I could hear him banging away with the hammer one day, and he was saying, 'This blooming 'Stralia, this blooming 'Stralia.'

'What has Australia done to you, Jack?' I asked him. 'And what are you making?'

'I'm making a "stairses" (stairs) to go bye bye,' he said. Then he got up off his knees and started demonstrating with his hands what he thought of Australia. 'This blooming 'Stralia's horrible, you can't have nuffink in this blooming 'Stralia, no "stairses" to go to bye bye,' he threw down his hands in disgust, 'nuffink at all, not even a blooming baby,' and he went on with his banging and his complaining. (That Christmas three babies had been born out in the bush, two white babies and one black one, and two of them had died in the intense heat. The baby that had lived was placed naked in a cot, after a sheet had been soaked in cold water and placed all over the cot; the cot was sprayed at intervals with cold water to keep it cool. That was the only way they could save the baby.)

Often, after my conversation with Jack, I would watch Jack

51

and Pearl playing in the paddock, and several times a day I would see them stop at their play and put their hands together in prayer, asking, 'Please, God, send us a baby.' Every night, too, they would end their prayers with the same request, 'Please, God, send us a baby.'

Now, back in Wales, every day was filled with new excitement for them, and they soon forgot to ask for a baby, but now that we were living with John, Mrs. Owen, who was many years our senior, started mothering *me*. She sent down a very large cooked dinner for me one day. I told the little girl who had brought the meal down, to tell her mother not to worry about me, because I cooked a dinner every day by the time Mr. Webb came home and the children came back from school. She said to me, 'Mammy gave me strict orders I was to stay and watch you eat up every bit of it. You are having a baby, and you must eat plenty of food.'

So every day I would eat two dinners, and strangely enough, although I always kept a good table at home, I always seemed to be hungry. Young Lilian would stand at my side and make sure I ate up every scrap of the dinner her mother had sent down for me, but I was always ready for the dinner I cooked myself later on in the day. Mrs. Owen was a very kind and loving woman; she adored children, and the more she had around her, the happier she was. She had four girls and two boys of her own. My children asked her one day, 'Why do you send dinner down for our mammy every day?'

'Well,' said Mrs. Owen, 'your mammy is going to buy a little brother and sister, and she has to eat a lot of food.'

They ran back to the house, very excited. 'Mammy, when are you going to buy this baby, can we have it now?'

'No, not yet,' I told them. 'Babies are very expensive, and we have to save up a lot of money before we can afford to buy one.'

Then they wanted to know if they were going to have a baby brother or sister. I told them that Jesus would be sending the baby, and we must leave the choice to Him. When "Daddy" came home, they were very excited. 'How much money have you got, Daddy, because Mammy's going to buy a baby, and it's going to be a very 'spensive baby.'

From then on, every Friday when Ivor brought his pay home, I had to arrange that one pound note and one pound's worth of silver were placed on the table, and to make more money the children would "gilly gilly". The pound note was for Pearl to

52

"gilly" and the silver was for Jack. Next Jack wanted a "Salsation" dog. His uncle Albert knew a man whose bitch had had alsatian puppies, and he had reserved one for Jack. As time went on, the children were getting desperate, it seemed such an awful long wait for this "Salsation" dog *and* this baby. One day I was looking over the gate at the children playing on the common, and I noticed that Jack and Pearl were having a discussion. I was able to overhear their conversation, which went something like this.

Jack to Pearl: 'Pearly, please let it be a boy.'

Pearl to Jack: 'No, Jackie, I want a baby sister.'

Then Jack, with his two hands outstretched like a beggar, explained to her: 'Oh Pearly, please let it be a boy, you've got lots of little girls to play with, and I haven't got one little boy for a playmate.' With tears in his eyes, he added, 'I've got nobody, please, Pearly, please.'

Pearl couldn't bear to see Jack crying, and at the sight of his tears, she said, 'It's all right, Jack, it shall be a boy.'

After that they went on waiting patiently for the 'spensive baby to arrive.

One day Jack came home and asked me to put a patch on his trousers.

'Why, Jackie,' I said to him, 'have you torn your trousers?'

'No,' he said, 'but the boys are calling me a "swank" because I haven't got a patch on my trousers!'

In the evenings, when the children were in bed and when Ivor was on the afternoon shift, I would sit by the fire and bring out my sewing, because I was making all my own baby clothes. I had to sew them by hand, as I didn't have a machine, and John Jones, who lived in the other part of the house, would come quietly into the room, take a chair and sit down near the fire. Sometimes he hardly spoke, he was such a quiet person, but sometimes, very gently, he would say to me, 'What are you sewing, Mrs. Webb?' and I would say, 'A flannel shirt for Jackie.'

It was always 'a flannel shirt for Jackie', but in fact I was making a back flannel for the baby. In those days young babies were dressed first in a little Chilprufe vest, and then a 'belly band' was wound round and round (these belly bands were four inches wides and very strong; they were wound round the belly button and fastened with a safety pin); then you would put a nappy on the baby, and turn it over on to its tummy on your lap. Next you

53

would lay a soft, white flannelette back flannel on the baby's back (this "back flannel" looked like a woman's apron), and follow this with a similar garment of Welsh flannel. Once all these were in position, you would hold them to stop them moving, and turn the baby over on to its back, after which you would bring all the tapes that were hanging from the back flannels round to the front and tie them into little bows. Then you would fold the bottoms of the back flannels (which were usually about twelve inches longer then the baby's body) over the baby's feet, and secure them with a safety pin on either side, so that the baby was enfolded in an envelope. Next you would take a long baby's binder, about six inches in width, and rolled up, and commence to wind this around the baby's body, finally securing it with a pin, or in some cases two pins.

For indoors or night time you would then put a long winceyette nightgown on the baby; this came right down over its toes. But if you were taking the baby out, it would first be dressed in a long petticoat of fine lawn or flannelette, over which it would wear a long silk or cotton embroidered gown. (The long the gown, the more stylish it was, and the prouder the mother would feel.) You would have six sets of everything, three for night and three for daytime use.

On Saturday, October 21st, the district nurse came round to see me. (In those days she was called "the Queen's nurse", and you had to pay two and sixpence—$12\frac{1}{2}$p—a week if you wanted her to attend you.) She told me I would need to get a large roll of cotton wool and a large bottle of olive oil. I asked her why, and she said, 'Oh my dear, we are going to have to wash your baby in olive oil and wrap it in cotton wool; it's a rabbit you're having, not a baby!' So then I asked her if the baby was going to be very small, and she said, 'If you have a six-pound baby, you'll be very lucky.'

I thought this was because of something that had happened a month previously. Ivor had asked me to have hot water ready for him to have a bath, and to have his breakfast ready by the time he got home from work, because he wanted to go up to Caerau. He said Ted Mannings would be calling for him, as they were going to sell his father's shed and its contents. That night it played on my mind that I would have to be up earlier than usual, and when I heard a sharp knock on the door, it was only in my imagination. I thought I had overslept, and that this was Ivor, come home before

I had got anything ready for him. I couldn't have been properly awake, because when I jumped out of bed and opened our bedroom door, I rolled all the way down the stairs. I picked myself up and opened the front door, but there was no-one there.

'Are you all right, Mrs. Webb?' Mr. Jones called out, very frightened.

'Yes, I'm fine, Mr. Jones,' I answered.

Ivor had gone straight to Caerau on his motor bike, and brought Ted, his brother-in-law, back with him. When they came in, Ivor's breakfast was on the table and his water was hot for his bath. It was very early in the morning, and I decided to go back to bed, but first I had to sit on the stairs to gather my strength before going up to the bedroom, and from there I could hear Ivor and Ted talking about the sale of the business premises in Tonna Road. I opened the living room door, so that they would know I had overheard what they had been discussing.

'Ivor, why are you deceiving me?' I asked. 'I thought it was your father's shed on the black tip that you were selling; but you are talking about selling the business in Tonna Road.'

'Oh Ray,' said Ted, 'I persuaded Ivor to get rid of the old place. He's got a lot on his mind, but he's seen sense at last, and agreed to get rid of it.'

I turned on Ted, and asked, 'What do you know of Ivor's affairs that I don't? Does he confide in you more than he does in me? What troubles have you got, Ivor, more than I already have to bear? I agreed to take two pounds a week, and that has to keep the four of us and help prepare for the baby that's coming. I have to build a new home and pay the running cost of the four rooms, all out of two pounds a week, in order that our debts can all be payed within a year.—That was the hundred and twenty five pounds that your wife and her brother kindly lent us, Ted.—You told me, Ivor, that you would never work on the hard ground again, but now you are, and earning fabulous money. You sold your half of the house in Carmen Street to your brother Tom, and that should have covered all your debts. Yet out of all the money you are earning, you give me two pounds. What are you doing with the rest of the money? I'll tell you.

'You bought one of the most expensive bikes on the market, and you paid an extra fifty pounds for a special pillion seat—for whom? You knew I would never be able to use it. You get the rent from Bryn Glas, and every quarter you get a big cheque from

55

the Co-operative for the rent, as well as the third of their rent from the Co-op's sub-tenants. I fought for that, and the money should be mine, but you get it. The Co-operative pays the rates for Ninety Tonna Road, so you have no worries there. Property is a money-making business for you—I go to Bridgend every quarter to change the cheque for you, so I know how much you are having. Now, Ted, how is Ivor in this hole that you want to get him out of? When I came back from Australia, I was penniless, with two small children. I walked sixteen miles to get work to keep me and the children.'

While I was saying all this, Ivor did not utter one word. I went on.

'The solicitor wanted to buy Ninety Tonna Road for the Co-operative, and offered me two hundred pounds; I could have sold the property and used the money to make life easier for the children and myself. You *had* authorized me to sell. But the Co-operative's lease had three more years to run. They would only have paid two hundred pounds for the property, and then you would have lost three hundred pounds in rent, plus the rates for three years. And now, when you've got more money than you have ever handled in your life, you want to throw that property away because Ted advises you to do it. If Ted is so anxious to sell property, let him sell his own—he has three houses to sell! There is still one hundred and fifty pounds due to you, if you can wait until the three years are up, and *then* you can think of selling it. And while we've got that property, we'll always have something we can sell when we need it—need it more than you do at the moment. Your father kept that property for you so that you would have something to give to your children—and remember you will soon have three children to keep. And what's more, thanks to the way you two were deceiving me, and because I was in a hurry to get things prepared early for you, I fell down the stairs, and perhaps I've killed our child.'

At last Ivor spoke. 'Ray is right, Ted, she has shown me just what a fool I look through her eyes. I'll run you back to Caerau when you're ready, Ted, but there won't be a sale.'

'Everything has been agreed, Ivor,' Ted said to him. 'You can't back out now, they are just waiting for you to sign.'

But Ivor was firm now, and there was no sale.

*   *   *

On the Monday following the district nurse's visit, the children were being got ready for school and Ivor was at work; the snow was deep on the ground. I could feel it was time, and I had to call Jack and tell him to be a big man and go down and get the nurse. He went to her, and she sent him a little further on to fetch Mrs. Meredith, who was to look after me and my home. When they came up, I cooked breakfast for them and the children, then the children were sent off to school. It was an effort to cook the breakfast, because the pains were coming very quickly now, but the nurse insisted that I carried on.

At twelve o'clock Mrs. Owen, who had been pacing up and down outside, decided it would be better for her to fetch the children from school and take them to her house. She didn't take them the usual way, because she didn't want them to pass my house and hear any sounds that might come through the open window; instead she took them on a detour. Mrs. Meredith kept asking the nurse if she should send for the doctor, but the nurse was adamant. 'No, no,' she said. 'I've never sent for a doctor for any of my deliveries, and this one won't best me.'

At one o'clock Mrs. Owen came to the house, to ask if she should send the children back to school, and she was asked to bring the children in to see me first. When the children arrived, they were told to go upstairs as their Mammy had a surprise for them, and when they saw their new brother, they were delighted. Pearl gave him a big kiss, and ran down the stairs to Mrs. Owen, shouting at the top of her voice, 'Oh Mrs. Owen! We've got the beautifullest baby in all the world!' Then she ran back for another kiss with her baby brother.

The children went back to school, and Pearl saw that Mr. Griffiths had changed his tie from the one he had been wearing in the morning, and now he was also wearing a new buttonhole. 'Why have you changed your tie and your buttonhole, Mr. Griffiths?' she asked him.

'Pearly,' he said, 'it's because you have had the beautifullest baby boy in the world today, and *I* have the beautifullest girl!'

Mr. Griffiths and his wife lived at Coity Cross. They had buried three babies and were overjoyed that this one seemed well and healthy.

After school Pearl and Jack came running home as fast as the snow would allow them to, and they came upstairs, bubbling with excitement. Jack was elected spokesman. 'We're very happy,

57

Mammy,' he said. 'Mr. Griffiths has got a beautiful baby girl,' and then Pearl bubbled in, 'And he's got a new red tie and a red buttonhole, and we are very happy for him, Mammy, are you happy too?'

'Of course,' I said.

The S.S. "Hobsons Bay". The ship we came home on.

Pearl, Jack and fellow-passengers on board ship – competition: "funniest faces!"

Rachel Ann Webb and daughter, Pearl, 1929, Western Australia.

Rachel Ann Webb the Author, outside her home in Western Australia called, "Caerau Cottage".

Rachel Ann Webb with Pearl and Jack in Australia, Winter, 1928.

Pearl, Jack and cousin Ray
on one of their Sunday
School days.

My sister Emily under a
Boab-ab tree in Western
Australia.

Me feeding a goat on
bread. One of the boys
working here with me. We
have 70 goats.

TEN

The next morning, when Ivor came home from work, John Jones opened the door to let him in, and told him to fetch the doctor quickly because I had been ill all night; he had heard me from his room. Ivor met Mrs. Meredith on the track, and asked her to 'phone for Dr. Trevlin in Tondu. Shortly afterwards she returned with the nurse, and when Ivor asked where the doctor was, the nurse told him that this was her case, and she'd handle it herself. There was no need for alarm, she said, and went home quite happy after attending to me.

That evening Jack came home with his arm around Pearl's shoulders; she was breaking her heart. He brought her upstairs, and she was sobbing bitterly. 'Mammy, please kiss Pearly's tears away,' he said. 'She's very sad.' So I had to kiss each eye in turn, and then Jack said, 'And will you kiss my tears away too, 'cause I'm very sad.'

I said to them, 'Now I've kissed the tears away for both of you, so tell me what has made you so sad. I thought you were happy now that you have a baby brother.'

Jack said, 'Poor Mr. Griffiths's baby girl has died, Mammy.'

Little Pearl chimed in, 'And poor Mr. Griffiths has got a black tie on, and he hasn't got a buttonhole, and he's very sad.'

Then Jack pulled himself up to his full height, stretched out his arms to his baby brother who had been so expensive, and said, 'Well, Mammy, what can you expect, they *will* buy cheap goods!' I had to bend my head down over the baby, not for him to see me laugh. I would have hurt him dreadfully otherwise, because he was such a "big man".

The next morning Ivor insisted that Mrs. Meredith should call the doctor. She was not to tell the nurse, but to go straight for the doctor, because I had had a worse night than the one before; but again she came back with the midwife, not the doctor. The two women came upstairs, and worked hard with warm water, which they called a "douche". Meanwhile Ivor got on his bike and went down to Tondu himself to fetch the doctor.

I hear the nurse say, 'Get a newspaper quick, and stir the fire up into a big blaze. Thank God it's come on the last drop.'

I knew it was something big, but she didn't say what it was. I heard the rustle of paper as she wrapped it up into a parcel, and then she said to Mrs. Meredith, 'Run downstairs with this and put it into the middle of the fire, and don't you leave it until every bit of it has burned right through.'

Just as Mrs. Meredith had finished stoking the parcel into the fire, Ivor returned with the doctor, and the nurse was caught out. The doctor asked her what it was that she had taken away, and she said it was a misconception of twins. He questioned her again, and she had to admit it had mortified.

'What have you done with it?' he asked. 'You've kept it for me to see, I hope.'

'No, I've burned it,' answered the nurse.

'How dare you burn it!' he said angrily. 'That should have been kept for me to see, and why didn't you send for me before? You've risked this patient's life, just to put another feather in your cap. And this patient has got septicaemia after childbirth, how do you account for that? This case will be reported, Nurse, and then there will be no more feathers in your cap.'

She was ordered out of the house, and it was revealed that another of her patients, who had given birth to twins at about the same time that my own baby had been born, had died as a result of this septicaemia after childbirth, leaving a husband and four little children. A third patient also died from septicaemia; she was a local girl from the village. Investigation proved that this nurse had been receiving fairly large sums of money to go in daily and treat and dress a badly septic ulcered leg, when she knew full well that she shouldn't have gone within a mile of anyone with septic ulcers when she was attending women at childbirth.

The next day it was discovered that my child was peeling. He must have been suffering from scarlet fever, and was now getting over it. A fever doctor from the local fever hospital was now called in, and he diagnosed that we were both suffering from scarlet fever, and said that I would have to be removed at once to Cefn Hirgoed Hospital. We were told that the children must move right away from the valley, so my mother took Pearl to live with her in a nice flat in Tonna Road, Caerau, where they were now living, and Elizabeth Anne Webb came down and took Jack to her home, to

60

live with her and Ivor's brother Will and their two boys. It was goodbye to my two little ones for six weeks. They had never been parted with me before, and now they were going to be away from me for a very long time.

The ambulance duly arrived at the door, but only with great difficulty and after having to make a detour round the common. The ambulance men brought the stretcher up into the bedroom. There were two nurses in attendance, and they waited downstairs, taking particulars from Ivor. I asked the men to wait while I wrapped my baby in a blanket, but they said they weren't taking the baby. At that I said to them, 'If you are not taking my baby, you are not taking me.'

The ambulance men called the nurses up, and explained what was happening, and they said, 'We can't take the baby, he has to stay at home; but we must take you.'

I refused to go, and they had to go back without me. I told them to tell the matron that she was my staff nurse when I was a trainee nurse in Blackmill Hospital. 'And tell her,' I said, 'if she can't take me up as a coach case, then, after five years in the nursing profession as a fever nurse, I have enough skill to know my baby will die if it is left at home to be cared for by unskilled hands.'

One of the nurses said, 'Well, your baby is going to die in any case, you can't expect a five-day-old child to get over scarlet fever.'

'If I am left to nurse my own baby, it will not die,' I told her. 'I will keep it alive. but without me, it will surely die.'

They went back to the hospital, but the matron sent them hotfoot back again, insisting that I came into hospital. The nurses tried to bribe me by telling me that they had given Matron my message, and she was delighted to know that "Tiny" (my old nickname) was going to be her patient; she had ordered a special ward to be got ready for me, and I would receive V.I.P. treatment.

'What good will all that fuss be to me, if my baby has to die so that I can live in comfort in hospital?' I said.

One of the ambulance men 'phoned the fever doctor to tell him I refused to go into hospital, and he came post haste, running up the stairs. I was sitting up in bed, holding my baby in my arms, and I said to him, 'Doctor, if they take my baby in as well, I'll go, but I am not leaving him to die at the hands of an unskilled woman. I am a trained fever nurse and, given the right medicines, I know how to look after myself and my child. I will tell Mrs.

61

Meredith, the woman who is helping me, to nail a sheet soaked in disinfectant over the door, to stop the fever spreading, and as we live in an isolated place, I don't see why I can't stay at home.'

The doctor told the ambulance men to take the ambulance back, but the nurses told him, 'Doctor, we dare not go back without our patient—Matron will crucify us.'

The doctor said to them, 'You tell Matron Morgan that she will have a dead patient on her hands if she insists on taking her into hospital. Mrs Webb will be dead before she reaches the foot of the stairs if you try to move her.'

And so I was left in peace. But the doctor warned Mrs. Meredith that she was not to leave me, night or day; she was on no account to go home, but was to isolate herself with me for six weeks. She had no children, she and her husband were a middle-aged couple, and Mrs. Meredith seemed a capable woman. Still, she was also a very frightened woman, and kept repeating, 'It isn't my fault, doctor, I haven't given her any damp clothes or anything dirty to wear.' After the doctor had left, she asked if she could go home to tell her husband and to collect some clothes. I couldn't refuse her, although I knew that she would not come back, she was so frightened by the fever, and I was right; she didn't come back and I was left with no-one to look after me.

We had to send someone up to my mother with a message to her to go to Marie Jolly and ask her daughter Harriet if she could come down and look after me. Harriet had helped me when Pearl was born, and I knew she would help me now. My stepfather told them that the baby and I had scarlet fever, but Harriet said,

'I don't care what she's got, if she wants me, I'll come.' And so she did, and took over the task of looking after me and my home, and I could relax, knowing I was in caring hands.

The weeks went by, and no one was allowed in or out of the house except, of course, my husband and John Jones who lived in the other part of Croft House. Finally the six weeks of isolation were past, I was able to come downstairs with my baby, and I could send for my children. My mother came down immediately, bringing Pearl with her; she had experienced many exciting adventures playing out in the street with all the children of Tonna Road. However, when she saw her baby brother again, she was glad to be back home.

Elizabeth Anne brought Jack back. When he walked in, he was so overcome with happiness that he just cried and cried, though

Elizabeth said that he hadn't wanted to come home. 'We would have liked to keep him much longer,' she said. 'He was so happy with our boys.' Gwynfryn was a year younger than Jack, and Alfred was four years older. They were very strictly brought up, but the three of them had been very happy together.

After Elizabeth Anne had gone home, Jack said, 'Mummy, I'm so happy to be home again.'

'Why did you cry, then?' I asked.

'I wasn't crying because I wanted to stay in Caerau, I was crying because I was so happy to be home,' he said.

ELEVEN

Caehelig was a very wonderful place for children. It reminded me of my own childhood in Ogmore Vale. Our mountains there were bleak in winter, but we didn't mind, because in the summer it was a perfect paradise for children.

Twice a year in those days my aunt Rachael used to send us a large chest of beautiful clothes, left after her daughters. Her husband, Richard Rowe, was the owner/editor of the Swansea Post, a local newspaper. They also owned a grocer's shop and an off-licence off Hanover Square, and their three daughters, Polly, Emily and Violet, were the champion swimmers and acrobatic divers of Swansea. The three girls were the same age as my two sisters, Emily and Violet, and myself, and so my sisters were always well-dressed, but unfortunately none of the clothes would fit me because I was so small. Violet, who was younger than me, was big for her age, and so was able to wear all the clothes sent after my cousins, Violet and Emily.

However, although there were no clothes to fit me, in one of the boxes there was a lovely doll for me. I treasured that doll; it became my most prized possession and I was able to buy little pieces of material to make clothes for it. It was a bone of contention between my friend Maud and me. She was very envious of that doll, although she wouldn't show it. We were playing out in the garden one day, during the First World War, and Maud was in the bad mood that she was always in when I had my doll with me; it seems that she had read "Made in Germany" on the back of the doll, and in an attempt to anger me, she took it out of its cardboard cot and threw it away. I had to go and rescue it, and an argument arose between us.

'Maudie James, you are horrible, you don't love my doll, and I let you nurse her,' I yelled at her, and Maud, yelling back, said, 'And you don't love your country, Ritty Bowen!'

'I *do* love my country,' I protested.

'No you don't, you've got a German doll.' And so the argument continued for a while, till Maud said, 'Prove you love your country. Smash your doll!'

So to prove I loved my country, I smashed my doll. I was a sad little girl for a long time, but I had proved my patriotism, and there were no more arguments between Maud and myself.

*　　*　　*

A fortnight before Christmas, I told Ivor that Jack would like a bike for Christmas; I had been saving a little each week towards the cost of the machine. Ivor had been in charge of the home during my six weeks' illness, and between the nurse's fees and Mrs. Meredith's fees, he had soon learnt how far two pounds went. So Jack had his bicycle and Pearl had a beautiful doll, dressed in blue velvet. That was our first Christmas in Croft House.

Ivor had reared and fattened some nice geese on the common, and John Jones kept some pigs, geese and fowls in some sheds away from the house, so my mother came down from Caerau to pluck a goose for herself and one for us.

Albert, Ivor's younger brother, always spent the weekend with us, and one weekend he came bringing Jack an alsatian pup for Christmas. However there was something wrong with the puppy, and it only lived for a few weeks; but John Jones replaced it for Jack with a pedigree sheepdog puppy.

We named the baby Ivan Charles after his father, and John became his slave; he would spend every spare minute with the baby, watching him at bathtime and rocking his cradle at bedtime. John said it was the best thing that had ever happened in his house—Ivan was the first baby to be born there since it had been built. He wouldn't let me take the baby shopping, but would say to me, 'Go on, you go, you can't shop with a baby, I'll watch him.' It was wonderful to have someone so devoted to the baby.

Spring came early that year, and it was a beautiful spring. It was wonderful to stand on the common, early in the morning, and smell the perfume of the honeysuckle in the hedgerows, and the fruit trees and the mountain flowers. The air was so pure and sweet, especially after life in the Australian bush, with its venomous snakes and wild life, the millions of flies plastered all over one, and everything so hot and dried up. This sweet mountain air was heaven itself.

65

On his usual weekend visit, Albert brought his girlfriend with him. He said they were going to be married and he wanted Ivor for his best man and me for the matron of honour. I had a new dress and spring coat for the wedding, but I hadn't been able to find a suitable hat before news came that the wedding was off. Soon after, I was planning to take my baby to the clinic, which was opposite the school in Bryncethin. The children were in school, but I knew that Pearl always kept a box of hats which she used for playing "Mother's House" with Jack, so I looked inside her box, thinking I might find something suitable to wear to the clinic, and found last summer's toque, which had once been my favourite hat, and was now a good match for my new coat.

So for the first time I took my baby to the clinic, which was held in the hall right opposite the school gates. After the clinic, as I was coming out of the gate, the children were coming out of school, and I could see Pearl, arm in arm with two teachers. She had lost the tomboy ways she had learnt while living in Caerau, and was now once again the pampered pet of the school. I waited at the gate to collect the children and take them home, and when Pearl recognized me, she loosened her arms from the teachers and, pointing at me, said, 'Mammy, Mammy, whose coat have you got on? And where did you get that hat?' I laughed—but I wondered what the teachers must have thought!

When Albert came to visit us at the weekend, he usually arrived after dinner on the Saturday. Although my hair was in baby curls round my face, it had quite long at the back and I had pinned it back in a bun. The first thing that Albert would do when he came in was to catch my bun in one hand, grab the hilt of a knife in the other, and pretend to cut off the bun. This particular morning I had had my hair cut, but before he cut it, Ivor had made a long plait and tied it securely; then, after cutting it off, he gave the plait to me. When Ivor heard Albert's motor bike stop outside the gate, he said, 'Quick, put your plait on for Albert.' Quickly I pinned the plait into my hair, and had it fixed just in time.

As Albert came through the door, he grabbed my bun and the knife (which had been "conveniently" put there for him), and then slashed at the bun—which came off in his hand! The colour drained from his face. He didn't know what to say, thinking he had cut the hair off, and he was full of confusion, while Ivor was calling him a mad fool. He went through a few minutes of complete horror, until Ivor burst out laughing. Albert was still in a state of shock, and he thumped me on the back for teasing him like that.

Life in Caehelig was very happy, and I didn't wish to be anywhere else. Then one day I received a message asking me if I would call at a certain house in Bryncethin because the coal merchant there would like to speak to me. I went down, curious to know what this person could have to say to me, and found him asking me if I would like to have the tenancy of a beautiful villa that stood in a little cul-de-sac at the bottom of Moss Row. He had intended living in it himself when he built it, and named it Myrtle Villa, but it was more convenient for him to live next to his business. He had wanted to find a good tenant to live in his house, and he felt we were the best. I told him that we were quite happy living with John Jones; on the other hand, with three children now, I would soon have to be looking for a larger house, so if he wished us to live in his villa, I would be very happy to take up his kind offer.

It was a beautiful large house in its own grounds, and had a long side entrance with a path leading to a tennis court. A high bank sloped round the side of the house and the tennis court, and stood between the court and the orchard garden; the plum and apple trees shaded the tennis court. On the opposite side of the tennis court was a two-roomed, thatched cottage, and Ivor made one of the rooms into his workshop, while the other was used to store coal and firewood. It was a picturesque cottage which had once been the home of the owner of the villa, and at the back of the cottage was a lovely, well-kept orchard; around each tree were hundreds of little hyacinths. At the side of the villa, between it and the thatched cottage, was a large kitchen garden, full of vegetables (although the kidney beans were going to seed.) There were two brand new pig-styes, stone built and with their own walled-in yard.

Ivor was earning enough now to be able to pay the rent for this place, so I had no hesitation in taking it. Also, my brother Garfield, who had how risen to the rank of Sergeant Major in the Regular Army, was getting married to Evelyn Hall, the daughter of a high class West End butcher, who lived in Mitcham in Surrey, and he wanted to spend his honeymoon with us. I had not met my brother since we left for Australia, and Myrtle Villa would be the right house to welcome my new sister-in-law to. However, when I told John Jones we were moving, he was very upset, though he

67

promised us that he would help us to move down; but when the time came, he had been taken ill and had been ordered to bed by the doctor.

* * *

If we had thought we were in heaven in Caehelig, then this truly *was* heaven; but fate seemed to decree that I wasn't to enjoy much of this world's pleasures before misfortune raised its ugly head. The schoolmaster told me that the doctor had been to the school, and he wasn't happy about Jack's chest. There was a shadow on the lung, and the teacher asked him if I would like to have a word with the school doctor. I agreed, and went to the school to meet him; he examined Jack, and told me that he was suffering from malnutrition. I asked the doctor how this could be, because I had studied Jack's diet and he was very well fed. Also I had taken the child to a doctor in Llanharan, and told him that I was giving the children Radio Malt because I was afraid that their bodies were missing the Australian sun. I did as that doctor told me: I cut thin slices of bread, thickly spread with best Carmarthen butter (so much that his teeth left an impression on the butter as he bit into it.) I was also told to give Jack a quarter of a pound of butter once a week, and let him sit on the doorstep and eat it as if he was eating ice-cream.

Now the school doctor said to me, 'It's not your fault that your child has malnutrition, my dear. He had a poison palate.'

I took Jack to Dr. Trevlin Jones in Tondu, and he gave me a letter to take to a dentist in Bridgend. The dentist had been struck off the register, but he was a highly qualified man, and agreed to treat Jack. He was very expensive, but it was well worth it. He drained the gums by lancing the gum and palate with thin wire to drain the poison away. I worried in case he was hurting Jack, but he said, "No, he wasn't hurting him." Afterwards I had to dissolve Condy's Crystals in water, and every thirty minutes for several days Jack had to wash his mouth out. It seemed to cure his mouth of the poison.

Then I was told to take Jack to the hospital to see the audiologist, who told me that the child needed to have his tonsils and adenoids removed immediately—though the risks were grave. Everything Jack ate was turning into poison, and the doctor said that if he did not have the operation soon, he wouldn't give him six months to live; but he added, 'I've got to warn you that he's got one chance in a hundred of surviving the operation. The choice is yours. Go home and talk it over with your husband.'

The sister put her arms around me, and said, 'If you decide to let your child have the operation, I promise I will not leave his side until he is out of danger.'

Ivor and I talked it over. It was a very hard decision to make. Should we keep our boy for six months and then lose him, or risk the operation and perhaps lose him straight away? Yet if it had not been for my belief in the power of prayer, many a time we would not have survived the night. So I put my trust in God, and told them to go ahead.

The next morning we took Jack into hospital to have his operation, which was to be performed some time during the day. I put Pearl to school in the care of Mrs. Owen, then, with my baby wrapped in a shawl, we hired a car and went off with Jack. When we left him at the hospital, we were told to go home, and come back at eleven o'clock, but though we left the hospital, we didn't go home, we walked the streets of Bridgend until it was time to return. Ivor suggested that I buy myself a new hat. He knew I loved pretty hats, and he thought a new one would buck me up. We looked at several hat shops, but my eyes were so full of unshed tears that all I could see was colours floating on water. I wasn't interested in hats.

Then Ivor suggested that I go into a hair salon and have a hair-do, but I wanted nothing, not even a cup of tea. All my thoughts were with my little boy, and I prayed to God that he would guide the hand of the surgeon. At last it was time to go back to the hospital, and the sister told us the operation had been performed, but it would be a few more hours before they knew if it had been a success. We went back again at the time given to us, and again we were told "No news." They told us to go home and come back in three hours.

We walked the streets for the entire day, too upset to eat. Then, to relieve the tension, Ivor went into a toyshop and bought a Hornby train set for Jack. When he came out of the shop, and told me what he had bought, I felt it was a good omen. When we went back at four o'clock to the hospital, they told us that Jack had come round, and if we went home and hired a car, and brought blankets and pillows, we could take him home. I left the baby in John Jones's care, and then, taking an eiderdown and blankets

69

with us, we went to the hospital and brought our boy home. It was a night of rejoicing. We had our boy home, and the doctor had assured us that with care he would make a complete recovery.

TWELVE

Now it was nearing Christmas—the first Christmas to be spent in our own home since we came back from Australia. On the 5th of November Ivor lit a bonfire in the large garden, and the children invited all their friends to the celebration; it was the first such bonfire that my children had ever seen, and it was meant to celebrate Jack's safe return from his operation.

(So that Jack and Pearl could invite as many friends to play as they wished, without making extra work for me in the house, we made them playhouses. The two pigstyes, which had never been used, were like little cottages; they were stone built, with a living room and bedroom, and were walled in by a "front garden" which would normally have been used to house the pigs' feeding troughs. I white-limed the ceiling and walls of each room and covered the cement floors with thick matting, and Ivor made some pieces of furniture to put in them. One of the "houses" was for Pearl to entertain her friends in, and the other one was for Jack to take his pals.)

For weeks before Christmas Ivor spent hours making a doll's house for Pearl out of a tea chest. It was an exact model of the house we were living in, and after the children were tucked up in bed at night, Ivor would bring it up from his workshop, and I would paper the inside, while Ivor painted it.

On Christmas Eve all the toys were in the house. Ivor went down to the "local", while I bathed the children, ready for bed. Once they were in their night clothes, ready to go upstairs after hanging their stockings up, we carried out our usual Christmas Eve procedure. I said to them, 'Time for bed,' and pretended I had forgotten that it was Christmas Eve; then they chorused, 'Mammy, you have forgotten Father Christmas is coming tonight, you haven't laid out his supper!' Then it was their turn to help me put a clean cloth on the table, and a cup, saucer and plate of our best china. Next I had to pretend that I didn't know what to give Father Christmas for supper, and they chorused, 'Salmon and bread and butter,' whereupon I had to cut thin slices of bread and butter and add some best red salmon. When it was all done to their satisfaction, they let me take them up to bed.

Shortly after the children were in bed, Ivor came home, with a big white fluffy dog for the baby, and while we waited for the children to go to sleep, we enjoyed the supper prepared for Father Christmas. Then, when we were sure they were fast asleep, we crept upstairs, Ivor carrying Pearl's doll house and I carrying Jack's Meccano set; but just as we were going to take the toys into the bedroom, Pearl's voice called out, 'Mammy, I can't go to sleep, I'm too excited,' so we crept back downstairs and waited again. That went on until two o'clock in the morning, so in the end we had to take the toys into our room and go to bed, but eventually, just before dawn, Pearl fell asleep and we were able to arrange the toys around their beds!

John Jones did not miss a day coming to see we were all right. He would just stay a little while and play with the baby, then go quietly home again. Meanwhile, Christmas passed, then we saw the New Year in and began to settle happily into our lovely new house with its beautiful surroundings, and plan to spend the rest of our lives there. Spring came, and all the hedges were ablaze with primroses and violets; Ivor began to think of turning his hand to gardening. One day he was out in the garage, attending to his motorbike, when I went out to the shed to speak to him. There was a man there, talking to Ivor about the motorbike, and I saw the contrast in the faces of the two men. Both stood six feet tall, and were fine, strong-looking men, but where the friend looked a picture of health, with his rigged outdoor expression, Ivor's once tanned face was now was white as a sheet.

When I remarked on the change in Ivor, the other man said to me, 'Can you wonder? Has he told you what work he is doing in the pit?'

'No,' I replied, puzzled. 'What work is he doing?'

So the man told me that Ivor worked one mile down, in the bowels of the earth, with a boring machine fixed to the head. The machine was electrically operated, and Ivor was a human bore, boring into yards of solid rock. A boy and a man to stand behind him, ready to pull him out if he should become jammed inside the rock, and all the protection he had was a piece of gauze over his mouth, to protect his lungs from the stone dust.

72

I couldn't stop to hear any more, I went into the house to hide my emotions. I knew Ivor hadn't been himself for some time, but I had put it down to an accident he had suffered some time previously, when we were still living at John Jones's house. Ivor and his friend, Jack Evans, who also rode a powerful motorbike, were coming back from Blaengarw one night, Jack leading on his powerful machine, and Ivor bringing up the rear on his Red Indian. As they neared the school in Bettws, some little boys who had stayed behind after the other children had gone home were standing at the side of the road, playing "chicken". They dared one of the boys to run across the road, between the two bikes. Ivor saw the children there, but did not know what they had intended doing, and he tried to slow his machine down; though he saved the child's life, he could easily have lost his own, since in his effort to avoid the boy, he had thrown himself and the bike across the road.

Fortunately the schoolmaster had been coming out of the school at the time, and had seen and heard what the boys were going to do, but he had been too late to warn Ivor. He helped Ivor up, and apologised for the boys' behaviour, then asked if he should call an ambulance. Ivor didn't want to make a fuss, he just wanted to get away, so he assured the teacher that he was all right. The headmaster, who knew each one of the boys, said that he would take each one to his home and tell his parents what he had been doing, and he would see to it that they were so severely punished that they would never play that game again. Meanwhile, Jack Evans had come back to Ivor's aid, and he insisted that Ivor get back on his bike and ride it home. He knew that if Ivor didn't do that, he would never ride it again.

They rode into Brynmenyn, but the bike wouldn't take the hump-back bridge because the gears had been damaged and the brakes weren't working, and it crashed through the wooden fence and fell down the embankment onto the railway line. The men from the Abergarw Brewery rushed down the embankment and pulled Ivor and his bike clear of the line just before the train came by; an ambulance was quickly on the scene, and brought Ivor to Bryncethin, though he refused to let them bring him to the door, in case it frightened me.

That had all happened six months before, and seeing Ivor looking so white and sickly in comparison with the other man quite upset me. Ivor wouldn't hear of me calling a doctor, so the next morning I made sure the alarm didn't go off to call him for work. I know that if he realised what I had done, he would be very annoyed with me, so I got up early, dressed my three children, and took them down to Tondu to see my doctor. I carried my sixteen-month-old baby "Welsh fashion" in the shawl, and we walked two miles to Dr. Trevlin's surgery.

Dr. Trevlin Jones said, 'Ask your husband to come down and see me,' but I told him that my husband would never agree to go to see a doctor—that was why I had walked all those miles with my three children, to beg him to come and see my husband. The doctor must have realised how desperate I was to have walked so far just to see him before he started his surgery (and I now had to walk the two miles home again), because he said to me, 'You go home, and I'll be right down behind you.' We trudged home exhausted, to find that Ivor was up and wanting to know where we had been. I told him, "just for a walk". He was just going out, and had only waited for me to come home first. I asked him not to go for a while, but he insisted he must go, so in the end I had to tell him that the doctor was coming. He blew his top!

I knew I had to use discretion, because if it came to an argument, I would never win, so I pushed him down into the chair, and said, 'Sit down a minute, I have something important to tell you.'

Ivor protested that he didn't want to see a doctor, and he was not going to stay in to see one, but I said to him, 'Ivor, you say that you love me. Now prove it, by sitting down quietly and listening to what I have to say. You love your children too, you say; do you want me to be left a widow to rear these children alone, or would you like me to marry and give them a step-father, because I could never rear them on my own?'

Ivor said, 'There's no man going to say he's had to rear Ivor Webb's children, that's why I went on the hard ground, and why I have been mean to you, giving you such a small amount of money to live on each week. It was so that I could save enough money that if I should die there would be sufficient left for you to live on comfortably with the children.'

So then I told him that was why I had walked all the way down to Tondu, carrying the baby and dragging the two little ones behind me—'because it was *you* I wanted, not money.' I told him I didn't care how poor we were as long as we were together, I had had enough of separation; and I said again that if he wanted

74

to prove his love for me, he would stay there and wait for the doctor. And so he did wait, and the doctor arrived shortly afterwards. He examined Ivor, and told him that he wanted him to see Dr. Trail immediately.

'You are lucky your wife persuaded me to come and see you today,' he said. 'If you had gone on working in the colliery any longer, you would have gone down one day for good. Both your lungs are encased in stone, you've done your last shift in the colliery, Mr. Webb, because I guarantee that if you go down again, you'll be dead in six months.'

Ivor saw Dr. Trail, who told him the same thing, adding that he was never to exert himself again, not even by putting a shovelful of coal on the fire. Ivor was very depressed to be told that he could never work again, because all his plans to work and save were dashed, but I asked him to think back to the tin shack he had shown me when we were out in Australia—the shack that was to be our home, out in the wild, with no inhabitants for miles around. We had weathered that storm, and we would weather this one too, as long as we were together. (We thought at first that we would be having sick pay and that, together with Ivor's savings, would enable us to stay in our lovely house, but we were doomed to disappointment again; when we applied for sick pay, we were told that we had been out of Britain for too long to receive any kind of benefit or dole from this country.)

Some time previously Ivor had come home from work one day and told me that he had met a man from Ogmore Vale who knew me, and had invited us out to his home for Sunday tea. He lived in Heol y Ciw, and we set off after dinner to meet him and his wife. When we got there, a nice tea was awaiting us in a lovely old-world house. I had expected to see total strangers, and was astonished at the reception I had. The man and woman in turn put their arms around me, hugging me and saying how very surprised they were to see me again—they were Mr. and Mrs. Arthur Evans who lived a few doors from my mother in Ogmore Vale.

Arthur turned to Ivor and said, 'If ever I felt like knocking a man down, it's now, Ivor—and the man is you! Why didn't you tell me you were married to Ritty?'

Ivor laughed it off, but I could see that Arthur was upset over it, and after a while he told me, in front of his wife and Ivor, what had upset him.

'I work with Ivor,' he said, 'and when he knew I came from Lewistown, he said to me, "Oh, I knew a girl who lived in Lewistown. She worked in Bridgend Hospital, and her name was Rachael Bowen. Do you know her?" "You must mean little Ritty Bowen," I said. "Yes, that's the one. What sort of girl is she?" Ivor asked. "If there is one little girl that we love more than anyone, it is Ritty Bowen: she is the best little girl that ever walked the Ogmore Valley," I told him. "There isn't a child in Lewistown that can't look back to happy times when Ritty nursed them. She've nursed *my* children when they were babies, and then she married some chap and went away to live; and when she was going, we said, "He's a very lucky man and we all hope she will be very happy with him."—You didn't need to pump me, Ivor, to see what sort of girl she was. You could have asked anyone in Lewistown and they would have given you the same answer.'

I could see that Arthur had never really forgiven Ivor for this. However, the Evanses came to see us at our house, and fell in love with it, and they asked us to let them know if ever we were going to leave it, so that they could try to rent it.

It would be terrible to leave our lovely house, and yet how could we hope to go on living there when there would be no money coming in to pay the rent? Ivor said, "We are staying", and I didn't want to tear the children away from this healthy, happy environment; on the other hand, when Jack came out of hospital, the doctor had advised me to take him back to the hills where he had been born, and if Ivor was never going to work again, how could we go on living in Bryncethin and pay our way?

It seemed that once again life had shown us its darker side. After all our hardships we had come out into the light; we had this lovely house, Ivor had been earning good money, the place where we lived was so beautiful, we were all so happy—but now the shadow was cast over us again. Fate once more raised its ugly head, and seemed to say to me, 'You've had your glimpse of heaven, now back you go!' and I was slapped down into the depths of despair.

We sat down and weighed the pros and cons of our future. Ivor said that all our debts were cleared now, so, thank God, we didn't have that to worry about. However, it was April now, and the Co-operative lease lapsed in May, so there would be no money coming in from that direction, while the rent from Brynglas

76

would barely cover our expenses, rates, etc. My illness and the baby's had also taken a lot of Ivor's savings and I had gone back to my two pounds weekly housekeeping (except that Ivor had subsidised my allowance for the higher rent I had to pay), but now, with no wages coming in, my two pounds a week was finished, and we had been told that we could not expect help from the government.

I told my landlord we would have to surrender the house, and asked him if he would consider Mr. and Mrs. Evans for the tenancy, but he said we were to stay there; he was not willing for us to leave the house, and offered to waive the rent until such time as things improved. Meanwhile Ivor seemed depressed and didn't want to discuss anything. He was content just to sit and wait for something to happen, but that was not good enough for me. I told Ivor that we had only one choice—we couldn't possibly stay where we were, and I wasn't prepared to impose on the generosity of our landlord, however kind he was; he couldn't pay his rates and other dues if there was no rent coming in, any more than anyone else could.

Ivor was not one to take too much worry easily, and he was no help to me in this matter. He complained that as the Co-op had moved out of the Tonna Road property, we had lost our chance to sell it, but I pointed out that he should be thankful that he *hadn't* sold it. Two hundred pounds would not have lasted us long in the Bryncethin house, and now we could move into the Tonna Road premises. Whatever they were like, the place was our own, we would not be depriving anyone of anything, and we would have a roof over our heads. Dr. Trevlin Jones had arranged that we should have seven shillings a week sick pay, but once again I would have to be the breadwinner. Ivor had bought me a new Singer sewing machine as a present when the baby was born, and I decided now that I would take in sewing and use the shop as my workroom.

Despite our difficult situation, Ivor insisted that he was not going to live in that run-down house to please anyone, but I knew that where I led, he would follow. Ivor's younger sister Winnie was a constant visitor to us in Bryncethin, so I gave her the keys of the premises in Tonna Road, and asked her if she would seal up the house—every door, window and opening—and light sulphur candles in all the rooms to fumigate the house, while I made preparations to move. Next I made arrangements for the van to

77

call and collect our furniture, and on May 1st, 1935 we said goodbye to our beautiful villa at Bryncethin in its lovely grounds, and hello to a delapidated, vermin-ridden hovel (as it then was) at 90 Tonna Road, Caerau.

THIRTEEN

Winnie had given me to understand that 90 Tonna Road had been fully fumigated and was spotlessly clean. When we arrived there, Winnie and her husband were waiting for us with the keys, but we found, to our dismay, that the place had not been fumigated at all. We stacked all the furniture in the shop on the ground floor while we sorted out what could be done with the house.

First we went down to the side entrance (down a road which also led to the lane and fields behind us), to see what the living quarters were like, and they were the most appalling sight I had ever seen. A large bakery took up the bulk of the land and when we walked into the yard, the bakehouse was on the left and the living quarters on the right. Structurally it was a good stone building, but inside it was filthy. We went into the living room, which had a stone floor; just inside the living room door was another door on the right, leading into what we called the "cwtch under the stairs". That was like the Black Hole of Calcutta, because it had been used as a coal house by the people who had occupied the top floors. On the same side were the stairs, which led up to the second floor. By the foot of the stairs was an open door, with a child's swing fastened to the frame, and about a yard inside this door there seemed to be a long cellar, but this was so full of filth that it had formed a wall which stopped us from going in. This had been the original coal cellar. Next to it was a big pantry, and a third door was that of what had once been a beautiful bathroom until it was used by the sub-tenants as a coal house. (Both sub-tenants had been colliers, so there had been two tons of coal coming in every six weeks; every space in sight had been filled with coal.)

The downstairs tenant had been an Irish widower with two teenage children, and the tenant upstairs had been a couple with what was then known as a "mongol" son (now we would say "Down's Syndrome"), and cleanliness had certainly not been godliness as far as these families were concerned. We couldn't put

79

our furniture in any room in the house, because the place was so verminous. I asked my brother-in-law to go up to the chemist and get me some sulphur candles, and he came back with enough to fumigate the whole street. Then we sealed off all the upstairs part of the house and put double the amount of sulphur candles in each room.

That night Ivor put a single bed in the room behind the shop, and four of us slept in it; he made a bed for himself on the couch in the basement. (We were afraid of bed-bugs if we put our beds upstairs). To my surprise, an old lady came into our basement, carrying a large tomcat. I told her we had a dog and I couldn't understand why she was giving me the cat, but all she said was, 'You keep it, my dear, you'll need it.'

We tried hard to sleep that night. I clung on desperately, trying to keep from falling off the bed, but the children were tired and were soon asleep. All through the night the cat kept jumping on us, and after shooing it away a few times, I called to Ivor to come and fetch the cat down. Ivor said the cat was already downstairs, and we realised that it had been rats jumping over us. That finished our night's sleep! Next morning Mr. Hyde, who was the local rat catcher, came over and offered his services. He killed seventeen rats in one morning, and told me that what had seemed like a wall in the cellar was an accumulation of filth that reached from floor to ceiling and went the length of the house and right underneath the pavement outside. It had been accumulating for years, and was a breeding ground for rats. The day before, as we were taking our furniture in, I had overheard some men saying, 'Poor things, they won't last long here, the B—so and sos here will carry them away.' Now I wondered, did they mean the people or the rats would carry us away!

The first thing we had to do was to clean the filth out of that cellar and destroy the rats. We enlisted the help of a few little boys in the street who were eager to help, and worked as a chain gang. I was inside the cellar, filling the buckets, and the children carried them down to the fields at the end of the lane; when we had removed all the filth, which stretched for some ten yards under the house, we laid down double strength sulphur candles and sealed off the cellar.

For the next six weeks, Pearl, the baby and I travelled up to Protheroe Street each night to sleep, and Ivor and Jack went to his sister Dolly; in the morning we would come back down to the house to clean. In those days the basic structure of the houses was wooden, and every beam had to be exposed to the flame of a blow lamp to kill off the bugs' eggs. All the skirtings, right through the house, were taken away, and every piece of wood was scorched black with the blow lamp. While Ivor was concentrating on the bedrooms, I was working on the walls in the basement. After cleaning out the filth, I brushed down all the walls in the old cellar, and when those were perfectly clean, I white-limed all the walls that went underneath the house. I gave them several coats of white lime until they were white themselves, and eventually it was like a white tunnel running under the house, completely free of vermin.

When we were absolutely certain that there were no more vermin or eggs left in the house, we papered the walls and painted, but it was still two months before we were able to put our beds in the bedrooms. It took more time again to get the house completely fit to live in, and not until we were certain that all the vermin had been exterminated did we take up residence. At last, however, after months of hard work, we had made our home spotless, free from bugs, beetles and rats, and were able to sleep safely in our beds at night, in comfort and cleanliness. The house itself was lovely, built from the best quarry stone, and we found the people around us very friendly.

Once the house was finished, we tackled the backhouse; this, too, was a fine building, but it had been left in a filthy state. The Co-operative had never used the bakehouse. The property had first been rented from my father-in-law by a Mr. Weymouth who supplied the shops in Maesteg, Caerau and the rest of the valley with bread and pastries; he had baked there himself right up until his death, six years before, after which the Co-op had taken over the house. They rented the bakehouse to a succession of bakers, but none of these had made a success of the business. The last young man they had rented it to had lived in the living quarters, and one night he had run into the bakehouse saying that the house was haunted! He went into the oven to sleep, but the door slammed shut on him, and it wasn't until the men went into the bakehouse the next day to look for him that they found him, still alive, inside the oven. That was the last time the bakehouse had been used.

Now we had cleaned it up, and we found it was a well-equipped bakehouse. When it was ready, we asked the sanitary inspector to call and inspect it, so that we could seek permission to open up in business, and he gave the premises a clean bill of health, saying it was the best bakehouse he had ever been inside. We engaged a baker to teach us how to make bread on a large scale for business purposes, and opened the bakehouse for public baking. (In those days even Sunday joints and puddings might be baked at the baker's, and not at home.) Tonna Road was one long road with no side streets or back streets behind it, so it was necessary for us to go outside the street as well as along it to sell our bread, but we gradually built up a round, and Ivor bought a large baker's basket which would hold two dozen loaves.

The baker stayed with us for a few weeks, but then we couldn't afford to pay him any more because Ivor's savings were dwindling rapidly, so we were on our own. Previously those people living in Tonna Road who made their own bread used to take it down to the bakehouse in Nantyfyllon, about half a mile away, to be baked, but now they were bringing it to us; however, because it was only the one street, there was still not enough trade coming in to keep the bake oven supplied. It was a very large oven and the public baking was not sufficient to cover the costs of running it. Despite this, Ivor was hoping to be able to sell enough bread, because now our rates were very heavy, and Ivor used only the high grade Spiller's flour, which was very expensive.

There were difficulties, though. We had no van, we couldn't afford a delivery man, and outside bakers had now started to bring their bread into the valleys, which meant that competition was fierce. When we first went out to the Australian bush to live, the Aussies had been very hostile towards us because they thought we would take work from them in the Depression, but the response we met with from many of the other shop-keepers in Tonna Road was equally hostile (and for much the same reason). It seemed that they were banding together to keep us out of business. The sons of two of the other shops used to stand on guard outside our front, and if any van pulled up outside our shop in the hope of supplying us with goods, the driver would be told to get on his way or be boycotted by all the other shops. They also tried to stop the people from buying bread from our bakehouse. One shopkeeper told me that he would buy bread from me if I would charge him less than the bakers' union price, but if I had complied, we would have been closed down by the union.

As Ivor was a sick man, there wasn't much he could do about

82

all this, so it was left to me to find a way of selling our bread. Our product was of the highest quality and the margin of profit was so low that unless I could get a bigger sale of the bread, we would have to close down. Ivor used to lose heart very quickly and become very depressed, and I would have to paint rosy pictures for him, to cheer him up.

'It's always darkest before the dawn,' I would tell him. 'We fought hostility and adversity in the bush in Australia, surely we can fight it in our own country. These hostile people have built their businesses on shifting sands, but we will build ours on a rock. As long as we stick together and fight this hostility and have God's help, we'll pull through.'

I knew that all I had to do was to get people to taste our lovely home-made bread, then they would buy no other; what was proving a problem was to find the customers in the first place. Ivor mortgaged our house in Bryn Glas for just fifty pounds, to give us a little money with which to purchase flour etc. I would have preferred not to have taken out a mortgage, but Ivor had gone ahead without telling me, so now we were in further trouble. Ivor was no businessman.

Now I applied to the Council for a reduction in rates until such time as we were able to meet the full demand, and I agreed to go before a tribunal to state my case. On the day on which I had been requested to attend this tribunal in Bridgend, I went quite unprepared; I had no idea of what they might ask me, and so I had no way of preparing my answers. I was called into what seemed like a police courtroom, and in the centre of the room was a very long table, at the head of which sat a man in an armchair, who made me think of a king on his throne. On either side of the table were seated eight men—sixteen in all.

I was put to stand at the foot of the table, a tiny figure, five foot one tall, weighing six stone, and in my early thirties. It was like being in the firing line; they shot questions at me from all directions, and all seemed to be speaking at once, so I didn't know who to answer. It was a frightening experience. I felt like a prisoner at the bar, fighting for my life, but I kept my eyes on the man sitting in the armchair at the head of the table. Before going into the room I had stood in silence for a moment, closing my eyes tightly and asking God to come into that room with me; I knew I wouldn't be afraid of anything as long as He was with me.

I cannot remember the questions that were fired at me, but I answered every one honestly and truthfully throughout, though the tribunal seemed to go on for ever, with questions and more questions. At last the man in the armchair stood up and brought the meeting to a close.

'Well done, Mrs. Webb,' he said, and came round the table and shook hands with me. I was standing there like someone in a trance, while he cut the rates in half and asked me if I could manage that. It was a great relief, and I said 'Yes,' and thanked them all, after which I went home, walking on air! Once there, I gave Ivor the good news, and it gave us heart to go on fighting.

*   *   *

That night, as usual, I went into the bakehouse to help Ivor prepare the bread for the ovens. Ivor made the bread and I helped by greasing the tins and weighing the dough. I usually finished in the bakehouse at three o'clock in the morning, leaving Ivor to do the baking, after which I would tidy up my living room ready for the children to come down to in the morning. We had a nice white-tiled bathroom where the filthy cellar had once been, and I would wash there before going to bed. (The basement accomodation was now comfortable, and consisted of a large living-room, a kitchenette, and a white-limed cellar underneath the stairs, in which we stored the children's toys.)

If I could manage to crawl into bed at a quarter to four in the morning, I considered myself lucky. My back wouldn't support me enough to climb the two flights of stairs to my bedroom, I would have to go up one step at a time, with my hands on the stair in front of me. Then I had to be back in the bakehouse at seven o'clock, ready to take the loaves out of the tins as they came out of the oven, and turn them over to steam. After that I would get the children down and off to school, and dress my baby who was now eighteen months old. The children left at a quarter to nine, and then Ivor would fill the basket with the two dozen loaves for me; he would then go to bed for a few hours, taking the baby with him. As for me, I would carry the basket of bread up to Caerau, and knock on doors, asking people if they would buy my bread. (I had to walk, because the basket was too big to go on the bus.)

By twelve o'clock I would have emptied my basket, and I would go home and prepare a meal for the children who came home from school at dinnertime. After dinner I would fill my basket

84

again and go out on the street, looking for more sales. Our bread soon acquired a good name in the valley, and I had no difficulty in selling it, but I had to walk miles every day. Fortunately my baby was such a pleasant, sunny child that he posed no problem, and when it was fine, I would take him in his pushchair, pushing him with one hand and carrying the baker's basket in the other. If it was wet, I would leave the baby with his father.

It was very hard at the beginning. I always felt terribly embarrassed when I went out with the basket of bread, especially when some of the hostile people at the top end of the road shouted after me, 'Oh! I thought you were a gipsy selling lace!' When they taunted me like this, I felt like giving up, but when I was near to tears my father's voice would come to me, saying, as he always used to, 'Hate and envy ne'er annoy, when there's love at home; in a cottage there is joy, when there's love at home.' My heart would lift and I would say to myself, 'I am doing this for love of my husband and children;' then, instead of giving them a spiteful retort, I would hold my head high and smile at them, and pretty soon I won their respect.

When I had sold all the bread, I would go home and make the tea, in time for the children coming in from school. Tea over, I would then prepare to open the shop in the evening. First I would take a seven pound tin of corned beef, then I would boil some potatoes and onions, and while they were boiling, I would make a batch of pastry. Next Ivor would bring any bread left over from the day before into the kitchenette and I would soak it all in an old-fashioned earthenware breadbin. After that I would line a large baker's tray with pastry, then fill it with bread pudding, and put another layer of pastry on top; the more stale bread left over, the more "Princess Pudding" I could make. Then, with the bread pudding cooking in the oven, I would make dozens of corned beef pasties, and then, while all the cooking was going on, I would clean up my kitchen and do all the necessary chores.

I would then have a wash, put on a clean overall, and open up the shop at about seven or eight o'clock, selling hot pasties, "Princess Puddings", and fresh tea cakes (which Ivor would have made in the bakehouse). I had no trouble in selling the pasties—people would buy them for their supper—and the youngsters would buy the bread pudding, so in no time at all I would be sold out. This went on for several months, and I also built up a good bread round.

85

Then winter was on us, and the weight of the basket made it hard going in the snow. Ivor bought a little handcart on which we could put all the bread and teacakes, thus letting me do everything in one journey; but when the cart was loaded up, I couldn't lift it—it was too heavy for me to move. At that point, the old lady who lived two doors away from us asked me if her boy, Freddie Lewis, could have the job of pushing the cart; he had just left school and she didn't want him to go down the pit, so she said she would let him do it just for a little pocket money, because he was getting bored at home. It was a light cart and he, being bigger than me, pushed it quite easily. Now, with the weight of the basket gone and someone pushing the cart for me, I was able to take my baby out in the fresh air with me every day. Not only this, but we sold more bread in less time, and with only one journey, while I had more time at home now, and was able to get on with all my washing and ironing and do all my household chores. Freddie was also helping Ivor in the bakehouse now, so it made things a lot easier for me.

Meanwhile Ivor had had to go for a "board", and Dr. Trevlin Jones told him, 'I don't know what you are doing, but you are adding to your complaint, so whatever it is, you must stop at once.'

Freddie was now able to do the bread round without me, and our bread was becoming very popular, but Ivor could not bake a larger quantity on his own, so we could only supply our regular customers. To take on any new ones would have meant buying a van and engaging a baker, but at that moment we could not afford either. However the travellers were now calling on me, and defying the boys who had been trying to boycott my shop, so Ivor gave me twenty pounds to start the shop going; we dealt with Diamond of Bridgend, buying sweets and haberdashery, and little by little our shop began to grow, though we had to keep ploughing every penny back into it.

One day a Mr. Thomas, from Cardigan Stores, Clydach, called at my shop. As usual the boys outside told him to go on his way, but he turned on them, saying he would put his foot behind them if they didn't get out of his path. While we were discussing the possibility of his supplying me with best Carmarthen eggs and butter and so forth, another shopkeeper (whose order he had already collected before coming to me) came out of his shop and called Mr. Thomas over. Mr. Thomas went to see what was wanted, and a few minutes later he was back, in a furious temper, his face as white as a sheet.

He said to me, 'I've met some dirty people in my time, but these are the dirtiest b— so and sos I've ever met. They told me they don't allow any of their travellers to patronize your shop, and they said, "You know us, but you don't know these new people, so leave them where they are." I told them, "Yes, I know you, but now is also the time to learn to know *those* people" (meaning us) "whether they buy from me or not." I'll never enter their shop again.' Mr. Thomas supplied my shop from that day and for the thirty-six years I was in Tonna Road.

Our business grew slowly and steadily, but unfortunately the doctor stopped Ivor baking; as a friend of ours, Mr. Tommy Owen, was opening his own bakehouse at the top end of Caerau, Ivor helped him to start up his business by giving him all the necessary things from our bakery, and Mr. Owen became our bread supplier throughout the time that we continued in business.

FOURTEEN

One Saturday morning, when the baby was two years old and we were comfortably settled in our now lovely basement flat, a van full of furniture arrived unexpectedly at our front door. Next my mother and stepfather walked in, saying, 'Here we are, we've come to live with you.'

I was horrorstruck, and said to my mother, 'But, Mam, where are you going to live? You can't live in the room behind the shop, you'll have no privacy.'

'We're not going into the room behind the shop,' she said, 'we are going to live here, in this lovely flat. You lot can go and live upstairs. This will be ideal for us.'

I tried to reason with her. 'Mam, that room behind the shop runs on top of this basement flat, and with all five of us in the one room, we are bound to make a noise over your heads.'

My mother looked over at her husband, laughing, and said to him, 'Well, we'll have to put up with that, won't we, Dai. We have given our rooms up now, and we can't go back.'

And so they packed up my furniture and stored it in the bakehouse, then took over my flat. We had no alternative but to go upstairs and live in that one room behind the shop, all five of us.

Soon after that my baby became very ill. I called the doctor, and he confirmed what I had suspected, that the child had scarlet fever. At that, I told the doctor that this was Ivan's second attack—he had been born with scarlet fever. The doctor asked me if I was sure the baby had had it, and I said, 'Yes, Dr. Trevlin can confirm it; my baby and I were isolated for six weeks.'

'Impossible!' he said, 'he can't have it twice,' and he stormed out, refusing to notify the case.

However, I took all the necessary precautions, and soaked sheets with disinfectant and hung them over the door. (With a business to take care of, I couldn't take chances.) Just after the doctor left, Nurse Aubrey came in. She was on her way to a confinement case a little lower down the street. It was her custom to walk straight in to our living quarters, but Ivor asked her to wait in the shop until I came out. When I did, I explained to her that there was scarlet fever in the house, and I didn't want her to carry it to a new-born baby.

'Did the doctor say it was scarlet fever?' she asked.

I explained to her that the doctor had at first diagnosed it as scarlet fever, but when I told him that the baby had already had it once, he refused to notify it to the authorities.

At that Nurse Aubrey pushed her way in, banged her fist on the table, and said, 'Don't you dare to say it's scarlet fever if the doctor says it's not.'

'I don't want to be responsible for an epidemic in Tonna Road,' I told her. 'I'm taking all the precautions necessary to prevent the spread of fever, and if, as you say, it isn't scarlet fever, then all I've done is ruin a few sheets. That's why I warned you not to come in here. You've just left a mother and her new baby.'

The doctor called back the following day, and I showed him the baby's foot. It was a swollen black ball, and the doctor told me that he would have to make an incision into it to release the black blood. I was supporting the baby in my arms, and he told me to turn my head away while he made the incision under the ankle; but in the mirror I could see my husband's face contort with shock and pain at what was happening. The foot was bleeding badly, but it was red blood, not black as the doctor had expected.

When the doctor first told me that my child was not suffering from scarlet fever, he had diagnosed T.B. meningitis, and that was why I had been nursing the baby on a feather pillow in my arms because I wanted to keep his brain active. Now, when the doctor could see that he had evidently made a mistake by cutting the foot, he had to staunch the flow of blood quickly; he told me that there was no hope for my son because T.B. meningitis was incurable.

Then a very strange thing happened, which may be hard to believe, but is perfectly true. The baby, aged two, spoke with the voice of an adult; he looked at the doctor and said to him, 'If I had a bloody gun, I'd bloody shoot you!' Then he said to his father, 'Daddy, give me the News of the World, please, I want to read about Abyssinia fighting Italy.'

Dr. Jones was a young doctor, and he looked with surprise at my husband and said to him, 'You've been teaching him this.'

Ivor answered, 'No, indeed, he's saying things we have never heard before.'

Then the doctor took the News of the World and said, 'If you haven't been teaching him, let's see him read this,' and he opened up another page of the paper and gave it to the baby. The child read the paragraph that the doctor indicated. I felt sick with fear, and I know that Ivor and the doctor felt the same.

Doctor Jones turned to me and said, 'Lay the child down and leave him quiet for three minutes. In God's name, Mrs. Webb, let him die; he only needs three minutes to die.'

I picked my child up in my arms and said to the doctor, 'When you've got a two-year-old child, see if *you* can let him die.' The doctor left, but came back later that night to say that he had made arrangements with Maesteg Hospital to admit the child the next day. However we had to make a decision before taking him in. 'The germ has gone into the marrow of the left foot,' said Dr. Jones, 'and unless the foot is amputated immediately, the disease will travel, and that will mean amputating the whole leg in the near future. I have to allow you twenty-four hours to decide whether to let us go ahead with the operation—but it is his only hope.'

So that night we had to decide whether or not to allow the surgeon to amputate and save the child's life. We didn't go to bed, and Ivor didn't look at me; we were afraid of what we might see in each other's face. When the doctor came the following day, we told him we had decided—they could amputate. The doctor took me and the baby to the hospital in his own private car. I wondered why an ambulance hadn't picked us up, but I was too sick with worry to ask any questions. It was February 1936.

I was put to sit in the waiting room, in front of a blazing fire, with the baby in my arms. There were quite a lot of people in the waiting room, but my eyes were too full of tears to see them, and my heart too full of grief to care that they were seeing my tears. The matron spoke to me, but I have no recollection of what she was saying, though I guess it must have been words of comfort. The sister took the baby from me, and told me to wait; they were taking him straight to the operating theatre and I was to wait for the results.

I sat there for what seemed like hours, my eyes fixed on the door through which they had taken my boy. I could neither see nor hear anything. My body was tortured with terrible pains and anxiety, and while I sat there, I kept repeating just a few words silently,

Jack, Pearl and dog "Woody" in a Winter Scene in Western
Australia.

Northampton, Western Australia, 1928. Main street with Stocks Shop in background

over and over again: 'Please, God, let them bring my baby back to me, don't let them have to take his foot off.' I sat there for hours repeating the same words, and then, at long last, Matron and Sister returned, still carrying the baby wrapped up in his blanket.

Matron put her hand on my shoulder and said, 'My dear, we couldn't take his foot off, he's too dangerously ill, but the whole of the leg and the foot have been encased in plaster of paris, and the foot will shrivel away and destroy the germ.' Then, turning to the sister, she asked, 'Is the cot ready, Sister?'

'Yes, we have sent the other babies home,' replied the sister.

They took me to the cot, which was in a little cubicle all on its own, and as the sister was placing the baby in it, I said to Matron, 'Are you keeping my baby in?'

'Yes, my dear,' she answered.

'Can you save his life?' I asked her.

'No, my dear,' said Matron, 'no person on earth can do that. Your baby is dying of meningitis.'

'In that case, Matron,' I said, 'he shall die in my arms, not in a cold cot.'

Matron looked at me and said, 'I want you to know, my dear, that your baby is as welcome as any other child, and he will receive all the care possible.'

Then I asked the matron kindly if she would remove the clothes from him and look at his body. She looked at the sister in surprise, and said, 'He's peeling.'

I said to her, 'Yes, he's recovering from . . .' I got no further because Matron finished the sentence. 'Scarlet fever,' she said. They wrapped the baby up quickly, put him back in my arms, and called the doctor to take me home, which he did without a word having been spoken between us.

The plaster had to remain on for six months, if the baby lived that long, and I was warned that when the plaster was taken off, the foot would have shrivelled away. Meanwhile the fight went on for our little one's life. To keep his brain active, I would sing to him as I nursed him—singing anything that came into my mind; and my song would always start with, 'Please, Mrs. Webb, where is Ivan?' which was supposed to be children calling him at the door. I sang because singing is more soothing to the brain than talking, and I "sing-songed" everything. I transported Ivan by song to the beach at Porthcawl and to rides on the donkeys and the see-saws and other rides. One day I bought a soft, folding perambulator, and every morning, after putting the other children to school, I would put Ivan in his pram and wheel him around for hours, in sun or rain or any kind of weather as long as he had some fresh air.

I devoted every hour of my time, night and day, to my child's recovery, and my husband was left to look after the shop as best he could. My mother helped a little with the housework. After some weeks the child began to sit up and play, and take an interest in things around him; he seemed to be making a miraculous recovery. One morning, when he seemed to be fully recovered apart from not being able to walk, I was dressing him when I noticed an angry red mark behind one of his ears. I put him in the pram and hurried him across to the surgery in Hermon Road, which we reached just as the doctor was getting out of his car. (He lived in Maesteg). I called the doctor's attention to the baby's head, and he said, 'Take him home quickly, I'll be over as soon as I can.'

I went home, and soon after a Mrs. Coombes, who had been sitting in the surgery and had heard our conversation, came to the shop and told me that the doctor had been frantically phoning all the hospitals for miles around, giving a list of all the complaints from which the child was suffering. After phoning, he told the other patients that they would have to wait for his return, as he had to attend to an urgent case. Then he came to my house and told us that he had contacted the hospitals in Maesteg, Bridgend and Cardiff, and not one of them would accept the case. The general hospital refused to take the child because he was suffering from scarlet fever, and the isolation hospital was not equipped for the kind of operation that was likely to be necessary.

Then Dr. Bell Thomas of Maesteg said that he would operate on the child, assisted by his son, Dr. Ralph Thomas; it was to be done at Maesteg Isolation Hospital with equipment brought from the general hospital, and an operating theatre was rigged up in the scarlet fever block. From the time when the doctor saw the child at the surgery, there was a maximum limit of twelve hours in which to operate, otherwise the child would die. Once again we were taken up to the Isolation Hospital; it was the evening of Shrove Tuesday, 1936 The whole building was like a beehive, with people running in all directions—such a scene had never been witnessed before in all the history of the Llynfi Valley Isolation

92

Hospital! The baby was taken from me and I was put in the nurses' sitting room to wait.

Not one of the staff, from the matron down to the scullery maid, went to bed that night. Matron offered me a bed, but I preferred to keep awake and alert. Hour after hour people came in and out of the room, and I kept asking, 'Any news?' but the answer was always the same: 'No news.' Towards three o'clock in the morning, I heard a motorbike stop at the main gate, and then footsteps hurrying into the nurses' home. It was my husband. Ivor was shown into the room where I sat waiting, and I had a terrible shock when I saw him. His hair had been jet-black when I left the house with my baby that afternoon, but now it was completely white. We couldn't talk to each other—we were too full of sorrow—and all I could say to him was, 'Ivor, your hair is white as snow.' Ivor was thirty-five, and I was thirty-three, but our hair had turned snow-white in a few short hours.

Ivor stayed for a while, but then he had to go because he had left my stepfather, who was afraid to come in, standing at the main gate. Then, towards daybreak, Matron came and took me down to the ward block. They put a white coat on me and a nurse's cap on my head, then I was taken in to see my baby. Dr. Bell Thomas and his son were standing at the side of the cot, and they allowed me to peep through the curtains, just to gaze at the baby's unconscious form. I asked if he was alive, and they said that they wouldn't know for thirty-six hours because he was on oxygen. Then they advised me to go home and rest, and have some food, and then return; they would know the results when the oxygen was taken away.

Matron told me, 'This operation has done more for the prestige of this hospital than anyone could imagine. Dr. Bell and Dr. Ralph used a solid silver hammer and chisel, and chiseled all the bone away from the side of the head so that they could remove an abscess that was only a hair's breadth from the brain. It was the most wonderful operation I have ever seen performed, and if, in the process of removing the abscess, one spot had touched the brain, he would have died instantly.'

I want to record this in memory of a very wonderful doctor, Dr. Bell Thomas, and his assistant, Dr. Ralph Thomas, to whom I owe a great debt of gratitude for my son's life. (Dr. Ralph Thomas, who is assisted by his son, Dr. Noel Thomas, is a very prominent doctor in the valleys today.)

Ivan remained in the hospital for three months before he was brought home to me, a little stranger whose memory had vanished completely. He only knew me as the nice lady who used to visit him every day during his stay in hospital, and he had to learn to know us all as his family. Three months later I took him to the surgery on the appointed day, for the removal of the plaster on his leg. Dr. Wishart had now taken over the surgery, and I was meeting him for the first time. He was ready for us, and had a nurse in to assist him. He asked me to wait outside until he called me, but I asked him if he would let me hold the baby while he took the plaster off.

He looked at me, and said, 'I'd prefer you to wait outside.'

'Dr. Wishart,' I said, 'you are afraid for me to see what you are expecting to find, aren't you?'

'Have they told you to expect, Mrs. Webb?' he asked.

'Yes, I was told six months ago. I will be greatly obliged if you let me hold the baby, because the child's foot will be perfect, I know.'

Dr. Wishart looked at me and said, 'I wish I had your faith. Why do you think the foot will be perfect when you've been told there will be no foot there?'

'Because God, who gave me back the child through all his suffering, has not given me back a cripple. That, Dr. Wishart, is the power of prayer.'

I still held the child, and I said, 'Go on, doctor, don't be afraid.'

The nurse nodded to the doctor and he commenced to take the plaster off. When it was all off, the child's foot was perfect, and the only mark on the foot (even to this day, fifty years later) was the incision mark underneath the ankle. The nurse and doctor were speechless with surprise, and Dr. Wishart took my hand and said, 'If there were more people in this world with faith like yours, there would be less work for us doctors!'

He remained our doctor and friend until his death, fifteen years ago.

FIFTEEN

The houses in that part of Tonna Road to which we had now moved had been built less than thirty years before by a syndicate of which Ivor's father was a member. They were beautiful large houses built from the finest quarry stone, which had been extracted from the mountains round Caerau, and they were the first houses locally, with the exception of Cymmer Road (also built by the syndicate), to have built-in bathrooms. When Mr. Weymouth, the first tenant, had lived at 90 Tonna Road and carried on his business as a high-class baker and pastry-maker there, the property had been very valuable, and it was only when the Co-op took over the lease and sublet to two tenants that its condition had declined. Now that the filth of the past six years had been removed, the house was back to its former state. Also, through my little child's illness we had discovered the warm hearts of the people of Tonna Road.

My two elder children had settled in, and taken to life in the street quite happily; though I was nervous at first because Tonna Road is the main road between Caerau and Maesteg. One kind elderly lady, who lived at the bottom of the street, said to me one day, 'Mrs. Webb, you have brought a very delicate child to live here among us, but don't worry, my dear, you've brought him to the right place. You will see that Tonna Road is a very healthy street, so let him go out and play with the other children and he will get on like a house on fire.'

And Mrs. Tirell's words came true; Tonna Road was indeed a very healthy place for children because they had all the fields at the back of the house to play in.

When I was nursing in the Isolation Hospital in Maesteg, we had many patients in from Tonna Road, and I got to know their families, in particular those of the small Irish community that had settled at the lower end of the street. In the nineteenth century boat-loads of Irish people had come to Wales to look for work in the collieries, and many had settled here permanently, finding

95

plenty of work in Caerau and Coegnant Collieries. Starting from the bottom end of the street at No. 110, there were the Caseys, the McCarthys, the O'Gormans, the Lamberts and the Hydes. They had large families, with many sons, tall, smart, good-looking Irishmen, and were a very close-knit community. They were a friendly and kindly lot of people, who took as much pride in saying "Cymru am byth" (Wales for ever) as they did in saying "Erin go bragh" (Ireland for ever).

I spent many weekends in their homes, and some of the happiest days of my life were passed in 109 Tonna Road. Indeed, I attribute my recovery from an illness caused by a smallpox injection that went wrong to the love and kindness of this Irish community. Sadly, now that I had settled in Tonna Road, I found that kindly Mrs. McCarthy, who had been "Mother" to everyone in the street, and would share her last crust of bread with any stranger, had passed away while we were in Australia, and most of the young boys and girls had married and were living away. The few that still remained there had helped me to clean out my house, and continued to be my friends throughout the years of their lives.

One day my mother surprised us by saying she had found a nice flat and was moving out. She said there was too much noise in the basement, from all the sounds of us moving around in the upper rooms above her head. So now we were able to go down to our basement and rescue our furniture from the bakehouse. I took on a young girl as mother's help. Margaret was a good girl; she lived across the road from me, and stayed with me for three years, until she was seventeen, and then she went down to the Vale, to work on a farm. (She came from farming stock herself.)

Then I employed a young coloured woman; she had left her husband who had been cruel to her, and come, with her two-year-old daughter, to live with her mother in Nantyfyllon. Evelyn was a treasure, and she was able to take all the domestic duties off my shoulders. Ivan was now a healthy and very happy five-year-old. He was very popular with all his friends, but he had one special friend, Alfie Penny; Alfie didn't work, so he was always around to play with Ivan. (Evelyn's colour was a source of wonder to Ivan and he was curious to know why she was different, so I had to be on my toes all the time to restrain him from asking her about it.)

Several times a day I would have to take Ivan into the bathroom to wash him, because he loved nothing better than to be covered in dust and dirt. Jack was always immaculate, but Ivan

96

was never clean! He was a perfect little imp, and when he was dirty, he would look first at Evelyn and then at me, and then he would laugh, but I was exasperated at the many times I had to wash him each day. One day he came in very dirty, as usual, and I said to him, 'Into the bathroom, Ivan.' Then I went on, 'Ivan, you are a very naughty bad boy, you are always dirty.'

He looked at me so cheekily, and said, 'Mammy, what are you bothering about? I know our Jackie is never "comfortumple" when he's dirty, and I's never "comfortumple" when I's clean!'

Fortunately he was a very happy, contented child who never went into tantrums, because on the day we brought him home from hospital Dr. Bell Thomas warned me that we were not to allow him to go out in the sun, or to cross the child in any way for seven years. Many times he deserved to be reprimanded, but we dared not do anything to excite him. We now had a wireless set, and my husband loved to listen to the six o'clock news, but Ivan would always be around at the time when the programme was coming on, so his father would say to me, 'Ray, try and keep him quiet for me to listen to the news.'

My husband would usually be sitting listening to the news in the sitting room behind the shop, and I would take Ivan aside and ask him to promise to be a good boy and just be quiet for a few minutes and let Daddy hear the news. We would look at me, with his beautiful blue eyes full of innocence, and shake his curly head and say, 'I'll be good, Mammy,' but he couldn't keep quiet. His intentions were good, but one minute of silence was quite long enough for Ivan.

Now when they were small I had told Jack and Pearl the story of Jesus being crucified, and the crown of thorns being put on his head, and I taught them to be honest and truthful because dishonesty and untruthfulness were sins, and when people were sinful, they were putting a thorn in Jesus's crown. We had another saying in our house too, which the children used if they wanted to convince me that something was true: "Ten fingers on the Bible." These words were sacred, a vow which no-one would ever break, and Ivan had learnt, like the others, that they were to be respected.

One particular night Ivor was listening intently to news of disquiet in the country and the fear of war that was in the air. I sat Ivan on the counter and said to him, 'Will you promise Mammy you won't make a sound while Daddy is listening to the news?' As

97

usual he promised, 'I'll be a good boy,' but I knew he wouldn't be able to keep his promise. I said to him, 'Will you say "Ten fingers on the Bible, I won't say a sound."?' Ivan spread out his ten fingers and said, 'Ten fingers on the—' but he wouldn't say "Bible" because he knew he couldn't keep the promise. Instead he got down off the counter and said, 'I *will* be a good boy.' The news came on, and he was good for one minute. I relaxed, thinking I had won him over, but then be began, very quietly, to sing "la la". Gradually he got louder and louder until eventually he was singing at the top of his voice and his father couldn't hear the news.

One day Ivan came in from play covered in coal dust and carrying his bucket and spade. 'You dirty little boy,' I said, 'what have you been up to now?'

'Don't "boffer", Mammy,' he said. 'I've only been helping Richie Penny put the coal in the cellar.'

'Ivan, into the bathroom at once,' I ordered. He stood in front of Evelyn, looked up into her face, and said, 'Don't "boffer", Mammy, I'm same colour as Evelyn now!' At last he had managed to get his curiosity about Evelyn's colour off his chest.

One day I bought Jack a pair of strong, steel-cut boots; his soft shoes had been wearing out too quickly on the rough roads. That evening, after school, he wanted to put his new boots on to go out to play. I had tried to persuade him to keep them until morning, but he begged me, and I allowed him to have his own way.

We had just had tea, and we were up in the sitting room with Ivor's youngest sister and her husband who had come to visit us. The weather was very nice at the time, but the nights were closing in early, and my shop which was double fronted and well lit was an attraction for the children, who played around it on these darker nights. (I had always warned the children to stay on the pavement and not to go on the road). Jack had gone out to show off his new boots to his playmates, Pearl was downstairs playing in the living room with a few friends, and I was getting Ivan to sleep on my lap when suddenly we heard a commotion out in the street and the screech of brakes. Ivor ran out to see what had happened, and his sister ran out behind him, while I got up and put the sleeping child on the settee.

I heard Ivor say, 'Winnie, for God's sake keep Ray back,' but I went out in time to see a uniformed man carry my child in and lay him down on the floor of the shop. I lost control completely and ran up and down in the stairs, wringing my hands, not knowing what I was doing or why I was doing it. All I could do was say, 'Oh God! Oh God!' and keep wringing my hands and running up and down the stairs. Ever since coming to Tonna Road, my prayer, night and day, had been "Please God, protect my children from the dangers of the road."

The doctor and the police were soon on the scene; they carried my little boy into the sitting room and put him down on the couch. I knelt at the side of my child, and as I did so, I heard the driver say to the police, 'It's a miracle, a miracle! Only God knows how this child is still alive. When I carried him in I thought he was dead.'

The man was the driver of the Thomas and Evans pop lorry, and was carrying cases of soft drinks. He had come from the Rhondda, and was driving along the road to Maesteg with his lorryload of drinks; as he was coming along Tonna Road he saw some boys playing. One of them pushed another one—playfully, but the boy had fallen under the wheels of the lorry. The driver jammed on the brakes quickly, but he knew he couldn't pull up in time to prevent the wheels going over the child's body. He tried to swerve the lorry, and brought it to a stop on the other side of the road, then got out of the cab, expecting to see the child crushed under the wheels.

Then he said, 'Oh God, I must be dreaming.' The child's boot had acted as a sprag, and instead of the lorry going over his body, it had pushed him to the other side of the road. The driver picked Jack up and carried him in, but he said, 'I'm sure his foot must be crushed.'

The doctor managed to remove the shoe, and though it was flattened, Jack's foot was uninjured. The police, the doctor and the driver looked at each other in amazement to see the foot unhurt when the boot was absolutely ruined. His body, too, was unscathed, and it was a miracle how Jack had been dragged along and not crushed under the wheels as the driver expected. Dr. Wishart closed his hands over mine and looked at me, and I was sure he was remembering the incident in the surgery when he had taken the plaster off Ivan's leg. There wasn't a mark on my little boy, he was only suffering from shock, and I knew the doctor was echoing my own thought, "This is indeed the power of prayer."

The next morning the police looked at the marks on the road

99

and they could see where the boy had been pushed along by his feet. However there was no case to be made against the driver because they were all agreed that it was an absolute accident. After a great deal of vomitting and a few days' rest, Jack was out playing with the other children again. Then one day a card came, asking for Jack to attend the hospital in Maesteg. There the doctor shook my hand and said, 'Congratulations, Mrs. Webb, you were right in not letting your boy enter the T.B. hospital. There is absolutely no trace of consumption in the child, and he must have been suffering from climatic conditions at that time.'

One day Queen Mary was coming to visit Maesteg and the shopkeepers were asked to dress their shop windows with flags and photographs of the Royal family. I was decorating my shop window when the telegraph boy brought me a telegram sent by Ivor's sister and brother-in-law, Dolly and Ted Mannings. They were now living in Stockton on Tees, and the telegram was to tell us that Lionel, the little boy who was born to them while we were living in Australia, had been killed. On the night when he was born we had been awakened by a terrible crash and the sound of splintering wood and glass; when we found nothing wrong in the house, we had wondered what the noise could have been—was it a sign of something? Now at last we had the answer—the terrible sounds we had heard, and that had heralded Lionel's birth, were the same sounds his poor mother heard that day, when she went to the school to collect her son and found a double-decker bus had crashed, and crushed her little boy to death under its wheels.

Lionel was betwen six and seven years old, and had a brother David, a few years younger. David was pining so much over his brother that Dolly brought him down to stay with me for a few weeks. She had relations living in Caerau, but when she had gone to see any of them, they had thrown their arms around her and burst into tears, so she said to them, 'I have had enough of tears, I came to Caerau to get away from that.' To me she said, 'You are the only one who has welcomed me with any pleasure.'

'Nothing would give us greater pleasure,' I told her, 'than to have you and David stay with us as long as you like. There is a time for mourning and a time for healing, and when you want to talk about things, I'll listen, but until then there will be no talk of the tragedy.'

Six weeks later Dolly went back, but David didn't want to go with her. Ivan was a year older than David, and in him David found his lost brother and his health improved. Soon Christmas was drawing near, but David still wouldn't go home. 'Auntie Ray's is my home now,' he said. His mother promised him all kinds of things to get him to go back, but nothing would make him change his mind. We already had our Christmas tree, and I had already bought my children's presents, but now that I had another little boy at home, I had to take him to Maesteg to buy some presents. I took him into Lockyer's, and let him choose whatever he wanted, to the same value as I had paid for Ivan's gifts, so that on Christmas morning they would each have the same number of presents to open.

There was great excitement around the tree on Christmas morning. I think it was the happiest Christmas Ivan had ever had, because he had his "brother" to play with. We were just about to sit down to eat our Christmas dinner—Ivor had carved the goose, I had dished out the vegetables, and the Christmas pudding was steaming on the table—when a woman I had never seen before rushed in, screaming out, 'Come quick, come quick, my baby is dying!' She pulled me up from my chair and dragged me out after her.

My old neighbour next door down to me, on the other side of the lane, had gone to England to live, and two sisters had bought the house. One couple had the top half of the place, and Ivor Collier and his wife had the basement flat. They had moved in a fortnight earlier, and the baby had been born on the same day. The Colliers each had a child by a previous marriage, but the children were not living with them; the new baby was a fortnight old. Now Mrs. Collier was going berserk, screaming for me to come with her.

I can only assume that she came into my house because my side entrance was open and in her fear she had run through the first open door, but I had no option but to go with her.

'Carry on with your dinner, and keep mine warm,' I called to Ivor, then I went with her, not knowing what I was walking into or what I would find. It seemed that the doctor had just left after telling them that the baby had pneumonia and as the child was so young, there was nothing that could be done for it, it was dying. I looked down at the still, small form lying in the cot by the fireside, and wondered what in the world I could do that a doctor couldn't. There were not many years' difference between this woman's age

101

and mine, and I had no experience in treating pneumonia. I could only bend over the baby while its mother screamed at me, 'Do something, do something!'

I prayed quietly; only God and I heard what I was saying. 'Heavenly Father, Doctor above all doctors, You have no eyes but our eyes, no voice but our voice, no hands but our hands; use my eyes and my hands and my voice, direct me in what to do, and I will obey Your commands.' Immediately God took over, and I knew what I had to do.

I sent Mrs. Collier to my husband to ask him to give her a tin of antiphlogistene, two packets of pink lint and a large jar of vaseline. While Mrs. Collier had gone on that errand, I asked Mrs. Gregory, the woman from upstairs, to get me a clean white linen pillowcase which I cut open; when I had it open, I cut an armhole and a headhole out of each piece, one for the chest and one for the back. I stood the tin of antiphlogistene in a saucepan of hot water until it had warmed right through, and then I told Mrs. Gregory, who was the calmer of the two, to spread it evenly on the two pieces of pink lint. While she was doing this, I took the baby, laid a feather pillow on my knee, and placed the baby on it. Mrs. Gregory had finished spreading the antiphlogistene thickly on each piece of lint, so then I told her to spread vaseline on the antiphlogistene to prevent it from sticking to the baby's skin.

The baby didn't make a sound. It could have been dead, except that I knew there was still life in it. Mrs. Gregory handed me one of the pieces of lint and I tested it against my face so that I knew it was safe to put on such a delicate little baby. Then I put it on the baby's chest and covered it with a thick layer of cottonwool, repeating the same process on the baby's back. Next I put the linen "vest" on the baby, making sure that the whole of the lint was covered, and lastly I tied the string securely.

I laid the baby back in his cot, then I studied him for a few minutes while I gave thanks to God. After that, I asked for a sheet which I used to cover the cot, so that the baby would not be exposed to the slightest bit of draught should a door open, or anything of the sort. I told Mrs. Collier to feed the baby in the cot; he was not to be taken out of it for any reason, but was to be fed and changed in it.

Then I took Mrs. Collier's hands in mine and told her, 'Your baby won't die, God has promised. Keep him in the same heat, don't go to bed but stay with him all night, and don't, on any

102

account, move him out of his cot. I will look in later on to see him, but I won't disturb him for twelve hours. I'll come in then and put a clean dressing on him.'

When I went in during the night, Mrs. Collier said, 'Dr. Wishart came in to see the baby, expecting to find him dead. I told him what you had done, and he said, "If you have put the baby in Mrs. Webb's hands, you couldn't have done anything better."'

I tended the baby night and day for the next few weeks, until he was safely out of danger, but it wasn't my doing, it was God's answer through the power of prayer. (When I hear people say, "I'm as good as those who go to church, I pray," I feel like asking them, "Do you know God? Does God know you? You can't know God unless you go to His temple.")

Then came the day when Ted Mannings came down. David had been with us for nine months now, and his parents were afraid that if he stayed with us any longer, he might forget them, so Ted had come down to take him home. The two boys were tearful all that evening and refused to speak to one another as usual. Ivan would say, 'I'm not speaking to you, David, you are going home and leaving me,' and David would answer, 'I'm not speaking to you, Ivan, you are letting my father take me home.' In the morning we went to Caerau Station to see Ted and David off. Ted was walking too fast for me—I had to walk at Ivan's pace, so Ted was a yard or two ahead of me; he was dragging David and David was pulling back.

'I don't want to come with you, I hate you,' David announced. 'Tell him, Auntie Ray, I'm not going home. I want to stay with you.'

Then Ivan pulled at my arm, saying, 'Don't let him go, Mammy, let him stay with us.

'He must go, Ivan,' I told him. 'Uncle Ted is his daddy, and he belongs at home with him.'

'You're a horrible mammy, you're the worst mammy in the world,' said Ivan. 'Everybody in the world got a better mammy than you!' He kept on and on, and we must have looked a strange lot walking up the street that morning with both children crying and pulling. I was glad when the train pulled out, because Ted had an awful job restraining David, he was crying out, 'Save me, Auntie Ray, I don't want to go, I want to stay with you.' Ivan kept telling me I was a "horrible mammy" all the way home, and to pacify him I bought him a car. It was very expensive, a replica of a touring car, but it was something out of the ordinary; it had everything a touring car had, even a windscreen and a roll-back hood. Ivan could sit in it to drive it and I knew it was a safe toy.

The car did the trick as far as Ivan was concerned, and his favourite friend was once again the sixteen-year-old Alfie Penny. One day, some time later, Ivan came in, clearly feeling very important. 'Look, Mammy,' he said, 'I've been earning money for you. I've sold my car for ten bob (50p)!' Of course, we had to go and retrieve it again.

SIXTEEN

One night Ivor and I were sitting, listening to the news on the wireless; things had been very grave for some time, and now we heard Mr. Chamberlain say we were at war with Germany. Jack was fourteen and Pearl was twelve. Jack had been having private tuition in engineering, prior to becoming an apprentice in Shepherd's Engineering Foundry in Bridgend, while Pearl was a pupil at St. Margaret's School in Bridgend, so we only had Ivan at home during the day, and he was attending school now in Tonna Road (at Tyderwen). We knew our children were too young to be called up for war service, but the news caused us great distress, after our memories of having lived through the First World War.

The street resounded with the cries of mothers who had boys of military age; they were all running around, seeking sympathy from other mothers similarly placed. I was very sorry for the mothers, but at the same time I couldn't help being glad that my son wasn't old enough to go. And, of course, the war would be over in six months, everybody said so.

One day a young man handed me a parcel and asked me if I would put it under the counter for him until he called back. I did so, and in the evening he duly called back and collected it. This went on for several weeks, until one day one of my customers recognised him; he worked for a company shop in Caerau, and each day he walked down Tonna Road, taking a short cut to his home across the river. One day he brought a double size parcel, and all he said, as usual, was, 'Put this under your counter for me, please, until I call back.' There was never any conversation between us.

My brother Garfield was now in command of Penlee Fort, Plymouth; he was a master gunner, and in charge of the heavy guns placed along the coast near Plymouth and pointing towards France. He wrote to me, saying that he was worried about his wife Evelyn and their newly born son, who lived in Mitcham in Surrey;

he knew London was not a safe place for them to be, so he would be sending them down to stay with me.

There was a great deal of activity at the time; people were being fitted for gasmasks, papers were being distributed by the Food Office instructing shopkeepers on how they were to distribute food etc., and trainloads of children were arriving at the small stations between Maesteg and Caerau. (These were the children who were sent from London to be placed in different homes throughout the valley; they were to remain there for the duration of the war.) With all this activity going on around us, we hadn't noticed that the young man had not called in for his double-sized parcel.

Evelyn and her baby were safely established in my home now, and things were comparatively quiet for that first year of the war. The Germans were staging a battle of nerves, and people in Britain began to think that there wasn't going to be a real conflict, but my brother knew the dangers—that was why he had sent his wife and baby to me. Meanwhile we were lulled into a sense of false security, though Britain stood alone, unprepared for war. However the military authorities were not fooled by the Germans, and were working hard to protect our country. Our little valley seemed very precious to us at this time!

Mr. Thomas, of Thomas and Son, Clydach, who supplied me with butter and eggs and so forth, told me that the Government had instructed them to release manpower for the Forces, and all the able-bodied commercial travellers were being taken for this purpose. Also, the grocers' shop in Tonna Road, instead of having their own wholesalers, were now to be confined to one supplier between them all; this supplier was to be Mr. Thomas.

One day Mr. Thomas said to me, 'Now is your chance, Mrs. Webb, to pay these people back for boycotting your shop and preventing travellers from coming in to do business with you. The duty of allocation of all fat, eggs, butter etc has been given to me, and I am the only one who can supply these people, and I will refuse to do so. The full allocation of all the shops will come to you; then you will have all the people's ration books and they will all have to come to you. That will put the other shops out of business. In this war it is the survival of the fittest.'

I told Mr.Thomas, 'I have long forgotten how they treated me. I have built my shop on a rock, so now I will not take my neigh-bours' trade from them, nor will I get rich treading on their bodies.'

Despite this, Mr. Thomas still refused to enter these other shops under any circumstances, especially the one he had quarrelled with, and throughout the five years of the war my shop became a weekly depot for the other shops. This was because I suggested to Mr. Thomas a way round the problem. I advised him to take their allocations in case he damaged his own trade.

'As you refuse to go into their shops,' I told him, 'bring their goods here and leave them in my shop. Then they can come here and pick up their goods and settle their accounts with me; I will give you their money as I receive it from them. The war won't last for ever, Mr. Thomas, and I want to be able to hold my head up after it is over; I wouldn't be able to do that if my business was at the expense of others.'

So we did as I suggested. It meant a lot of work for me, but at least I had the satisfaction of knowing I was doing the right thing. Every Thursday morning my shop was like a fairground, but the other shopkeepers weren't very appreciative, they seemed to accept it as their due.

One day we came across the young man's parcel under my counter, and Mr. Thomas suggested that I open it, since it was apparently a piece of meat, and if it had been left any longer it would have smelt my shop out. Mr. Thomas opened the parcel, and inside we found two large rolls of luncheon meat, about fourteen pounds in weight. When they saw the meat, some customers who were in the shop at the time said, 'Oh, that's just what we would like,' and they insisted on me putting it in the slicing machine and selling it to them. As each roll was encased in a red, air-tight skin, it was meant to last indefinitely as long as it was kept sealed, and in a very short time the fourteen pounds of meat had been distributed amongst all the customers. They told us they were usually only able to buy this meat at the shop where the young man worked.

Sortly afterwards, as things seemed so quiet in London, Evelyn and her baby went back, but then my sister came down with her two children, a boy and a girl, ten and twelve years old. Her husband, Fred Grant, was the only child of his mother who was the manageress of Pears' Factory; she was a very genteel person who devoted her entire life to her two grandchildren. She had bought my sister a lovely house in Smallbury Avenue, Isleworth, and lived there with them.

One day the young man came in again with another parcel.

When I reminded him of the parcel he had left with me, he said, 'Oh, I forgot all about it.' I told him I had sold it to my customers, and said that if he would tell me how much it had cost, I would gladly pay him for it, but he would not accept any payment. He just said he was glad I had sold it.

That night we heard someone rattling the shop gates. It was the young man, and he asked if he could come in and speak with us, as he had a proposition to make. The stores where he worked were a wholesale establishment which supplied most of the shops in Caerau, and he said that his boss had sent him down to ask us if we would like to buy fifty poundsworth of sugar. Rationing had not yet been introduced, and he told us that if we had the most sugar for sale when rationing *was* introduced, then we would have the most ration books.

When he was ill, Ivor had been told not to work by his doctor, but now he had been called back to the colliery for his war service. He was happy to be back in work, and never complained, although he must have found it very difficult to breathe, with both of his lungs encased in stone dust. The country needed the coal, all the able-bodied men of the valley had been taken off to war, and manpower was so short in the colliery that anyone who could hold a pick and shovel was assured of a job, regardless of his health. By this time my own health was failing badly and my heart was causing Dr. Wishart great concern. He called in every morning, on his way to his surgery in Caerau, 'Just to test that little ticker of yours,' as he used to say.

Ivor was working the night shift in the colliery, and looking after the shop by day, doing what he could to help, when the young man called. We bought the fifty pounds of sugar, but then the man wanted us to buy a hundred poundsworth of packet sugar, saying he would throw in a case of Nestlé's milk for good measure. He said his manager had overstocked, and they had no room in the warehouse for the stock that was coming in; hence he was advising us to take advantage of the offer he was making. We had no place to keep the sugar, but my husband stacked it on our stairs, box on top of box, from the floor to the ceiling. Then we stacked our white-lined cellar with cases of Nestlé's milk, all of which we bought for under the wholesaler's price.

The young man was very persistent, always saying that he daren't go back until he had sold all his goods. These came to two hundred pounds, which in those days was a lot of money. Soon we had no more room to stock anything, but still the man came down pestering us. Now he was offering large legs of ham, but as we had no fridge, we had to refuse to take most of them. I think by now Ivor's money had gone, but we felt we had enough stock to see us through the war!

One weekend we were without ham for our customers. We gave credit to our customers, and on a Thursday they would have what we called "turn books". This meant that their credit account books would be made up to the Wednesday, to be paid on the Friday, and they were expected to pay before having any more credit; however, they didn't always pay up, and "turn books" meant that all credit taken after the book was made up would go on to the following week's credit. On this particular Thursday they were all waiting for their ham, but it hadn't come down, so my husband asked me to go up on the bus to the wholesaler and ask him to put it on the bus for me to bring down. (The leg of ham had been paid for over a week before, but it hadn't been delivered, and we had been without ham for a whole week.)

When I walked into the wholesaler's shop, I expected to see a large store, but it was even smaller than my own shop. I tried to draw the attention of a man standing behind the counter, but he ignored me, and I assumed that the manager was out in the store room. Every time I tried to speak to someone, they would tell me to wait. It seemed strange that there were no customers in the shop, and I appeared to be an embarrassment to the people there; I was half inclined to come away and go back some other time, but then a man who looked very important came out, and I assumed he was the manager. I asked him if I could have the ham for Mr. Webb.

The man went into the store room, then came back out and asked, 'Did you say you had paid for the leg of ham?'

'Yes,' I answered, 'I paid the delivery man.'

'Have you a receipt for it?' he asked.

I said, 'No, not with me, but my husband has the receipt in the shop.'

'If I come down to your shop now, can I see the receipt?' he enquired.

'Yes, certainly,' I replied, and I went with him in his car. Ivor took the file down, and showed the man all the receipts.

'You've been buying with them for some time,' he said.

'Yes,' said Ivor. 'We got to know the young man through his

109

leaving his parcels here every week. Once he forgot to collect his parcel and we opened it and sold his meat, and that's how it all started. I understand he supplies quite a number of shops in Caerau.'

'Yes,' said the man, 'he does. But why are your bills so high?'

'Oh, that's easily explained,' Ivor said. 'He told us that you were short of storage space, and that he wanted to get rid of all the old stock before stock taking. Then with our money he could satisfy his stock taker and restock his store room.'

The man thanked my husband for showing him the receipt, and said, 'You are in the clear, Mr. Webb.' Then he bade us good day. He had brought the ham down with him, and after thanking us for our co-operation, he left the shop.

Then the rumours started to fly around that the manager had been taken to jail. How true that was, I don't know, but he wasn't seen around Caerau again. The next morning there was another sensation. At the back of the last house was a big black tip which led down to the river; this was the short cut taken by the young man after picking up his parcels, and that morning they found his body, hidden in a hole he had dug for himself in the slag. He had died from poisoning, a young life wasted.

SEVENTEEN

It was Easter Monday now, and the chapel congregations had all joined together for a Cymanfa Ganu (Singing Festival). Buses came to our chapel and I took my three children on the bus to Nantymoel, where there was a large festival. We sang for a few hours, then we broke off for tea and sandwiches which were provided by the Nantymoel church people. There were about twelve children in our group and they wanted to go out and buy sweets, but as the chapel doors opened out on to the main road, I wouldn't let my children go on their own. So I gathered all the children around me and said to them, 'Come with me, I'll take you down to a little shop that I know.'

We still had a little time before the festival commenced again, so, like the Pied Piper, I took all the children to a sweet shop cum ice-cream parlour which was owned by my husband's cousin, Kitty Richards. Kitty was just leaving the shop as we arrived there; she had had no business all day and she was overjoyed to see me coming in with all the children because she had made a new batch of ice-cream for which she had had no customers. The children all had plenty of money to spend and they kept her busy supplying them with sweets; they all ended up with a large ice-cream cone. Kitty showed me a new ice-cream machine, and I told her that I had never seen or heard of one before.

'They are marvellous,' she told me. 'You should have one, Rit.'

'Are they very expensive?' I asked. (I had been making ice-cream in the old-fashioned way in an old ice-cream tub up till then.)

'Yes,' she said, 'but you can afford it, Rit. The ice-cream will pay for itself.'

We went back to the chapel, leaving behind a very grateful Kitty Richards.

On the following Monday we had a Sunday School tea, and during the party a little boy came running in to me, saying, 'Mr.

111

Webb sent me down to ask you, will you come quickly, there is a salesman in the shop waiting to see you.'

It was the salesman for the ice-cream machine, and he said that Kitty Richards had sent him, and told him he was not to go without an order.

'Yes, I've seen my cousin's machine,' I said, 'but I could never afford one like that, and my husband will never allow anything to come into the shop on credit.'

'Kitty told me your husband would say he couldn't afford it,' the salesman agreed, 'but she said I was to put a machine in anyway, because she was sure that once it was in, he would pay for it. And your husband has already agreed that if you want it, you can have it.'

So the machine was installed, and I was instructed in how to use it; that was the best couple of hundred pounds we ever spent, since it increased our trade enormously. The salesman said that I was the first non-Italian in the whole valley to have an ice-cream-making machine installed. Soon trade was booming; the children of Tonna Road had no other chance of tasting ice-cream because the Italian café-owners, the only other people who made ice-cream, only had shops in town, and that was too far for the children to go.

The salesman had made arrangements with the Ministry of Food for me to be supplied with ice-cream sugar and margarine; this was necessary to make the ice-cream nutritious, something the children needed because of the lack of vitamins in the diet they were receiving now that rationing had started.

The Italians apart, I was the only person who had ever attempted to make ice-cream in the whole of Caerau and Nantyfyllon, but one day the people in a shop higher up the road, annoyed because I was doing this, applied to Walls, the ice-cream manufacturers, asking Walls to employ their boy to sell ice-cream in the street for them. The next thing I knew was that there was a 'Stop me and buy one' tricycle (a large three-wheeled bike) outside my shop; it was ridden by the boy who had led the boycott of the shop when I first opened it, and there was an icepack strapped to the back of the tricycle, holding pre-packed ice-cream wafers.

The boy parked himself outside my door from early morning till late at night, and when he went home for meals, his brother took over from him. He would ring a handball and shout, 'Walls ice-cream! Come and buy one. Best ice-cream!' Then, when he saw a child coming into my shop to buy *my* ice-cream, he would say to them, 'Hey, come here you, and buy your wafers from me.' The children were too frightened to come into my shop.

Many of my customers were disgusted about this, but, as they said, they couldn't prevent the children from buying from the boys. When my travellers came and saw what the two brothers were doing, they advised me to send for the police, but I said, 'No, I don't want to cause any arguments with them. Give them enough rope and they'll hang themselves.' But the rep who had sold me the ice-cream machine called in one day to check that everything was working, and he saw the 'Stop me and buy one' boy outside my door. He asked how long this had been going on.

'For weeks,' I said.'I thought he would have been danted by now, but it seems he is determined to ruin my trade.'

(This was their way of repaying me for being their main source of supply and taking in their goods from the wholesaler; I could have closed their own business down if I had chosen to do so, yet now they were determined to interfere with my trade because they were jealous of my success.)

The rep. asked me why I hadn't sent for the police, but I told him the boys weren't on my property, they were in the gutter, to which he said, 'We'll soon see about that!' He went out and said to the boy, 'Hey, you, on your bike and shift from here.'

'Not for you, mister,' said the boy.'I've got every right to park here.'

'Very well, then, we'll let the police decide,' said the rep. 'Mrs. Webb has every right to take you to court and sue you very heavily, and if she won't do it, I will.'

The boy wasn't long moving. Shortly afterwards he was called up for the army, and, sad to relate, he was killed.

One day a van loaded with furniture pulled up outside my shop; the stuff belonged to my mother and Dai, and I thought of the old song, "Off went the van with my old home in it—Mam and Dai followed on without their pet linnet." They were moving back into my home without a word of warning, and once again we had to give up the comfort of our lovely basement flat and move, all five of us, to the tiny room behind the shop, as well as facing the discomforts of having to go downstairs to the toilet, to fetch water etc. The "phoney war" had ended, and my mother said, 'I've come back to be with you, Rit, because Dai is afraid of those bombers going over, and we are afraid of being on our own in the blackout, so he suggested we come back.'

'Mam,' I said, 'you know it is too noisy for you with five of us over your heads.'

'Oh well,' she answered, 'we'll just have to put up with it.'

I was tired of being used as a convenience for other people. I had two other sisters and two brothers, but they lived away from the valley and couldn't be inconvenienced with the old people. On the other hand, I loved Mother and Dai, and if it was making them happy to be with me, so be it. It wouldn't be for long, and I felt I had done my best for them, but it was very uncomfortable for us. The children were older now, and we felt like sardines in that one room, as well as having to suffer the hardship of carrying up coal and water from downstairs.

By now German bombers were flying over Nantyfyllon and Caerau on their way to Swansea; they were devastating the town in their efforts to find the refineries. Every night, over the radio, would come the dreaded words, 'Gairmany calling, Gairmany calling,' as Lord Haw Haw gave us his forecast of what Germany was going to do to us. He even mentioned Caerau one night. People had been saying that he was wrong and the Germans could not attack us because the mountains were so high that the planes would have to fly close to them, and if they did so, the bombs would probably explode underneath the planes, so they dare not risk it. Then on several nights we heard, 'You people of Caerau think you are safe, but we'll get you, we'll get you. We know where your collieries are, and we will blow them up when you least expect it.'

When the siren went off during the night, we would rush down to the basement—now our white-limed cellar came in useful; we had put a few chairs in there, and a single bed in case anyone needed to lie down. We would have our gasmasks at the ready, and sit there listening to the dreaded drone of the enemy planes. All our windows were blacked out with black curtains and blinds, which was the law, and around our light bulbs we pinned a black cloth so that when we switched on our light it would shine down to the floor. We groped about in darkness in our living room because our houses, being three storeys high, would attract the bombers.

As soon as the alarm was given at the police station, the

114

collieries and the fire station would set off their sirens. The sound was terrifying in itself, but almost at once we would hear the running footsteps of the Home Guard going in every direction, and often we would hear a voice shout 'Put out that light!' at someone who had left a chink of light showing. We were living in a world of fear.

One night, when Ivor was at work on the night shift, and all the rest of us were down in the basement, it seemed as if the "All Clear" was never going to sound. We were all crouched in the cellar, and I kept on making cups of tea. My mother and Dai were terribly frightened; they had lived through the Boer War and the Great War, but they had never known such fear as they were experiencing then, with those great bombers roaring over us. There was little conversation; someone would say, 'Gee, they're a long time this time, aren't they?' then there would be a lull in the noise of the planes and my mother would say, 'Oh, thank God for that, now we can go back to bed.' (The old folk were always afraid that if the house was hit by a bomb, it would collapse on us, but they needn't have worried; the cellar in which we were sheltering had very thick walls of stone which would certainly have supported the weight of the house if it had been hit. Not even fire would get through those walls.)

Each time we got up, intending to go to bed, the noise would start up again, and I would have to make more cups of tea to soothe our frightened nerves. We had now been in the cellar for three hours—three hours of terror for the old people. At last, after dishing up yet another round of tea, I crept up the stairs to the shop to see if there was someone I could ask if the "All Clear" had gone. Then I saw what had kept us down in the cellar for three hours, and I went downstairs laughing and told them, 'Get to bed all of you, the "All Clear" sounded hours ago!' The culprit that had frightened us into believing the planes were still droning overhead was none other than our modern automatic ice-cream machine. The lull in the noise had come when it shut itself off, and the vibration when it turned itself on again was what had caused the ceiling to vibrate!

*   *   *

To give us more room in our little sitting room behind the shop, we had had the big kitchen range removed and replaced with a

115

small, modern, tiled grate. One cold, dark night my mother and stepfather retired early to bed, about eight-thirty, leaving me tidying the shop. Ivor was having his supper while he waited for the bus which would call at nine o'clock to take him to St. John's Colliery in Maesteg.

When my task was finished, I went into the sitting room and threw myself, exhausted, into the armchair beside the fire. In order to deaden the sound of our footsteps for the comfort of my mother and stepfather down in the basement, we had just covered the wooden floor with thick cork lino, but as we still had complaints from below, we then covered the lino with carpet; still the complaints came, so we put rugs on top of the carpet. Now, as I sat by the fire, I took my slippers off to ease my tired, burning feet—only to find that the floor was burning my bare feet. I felt a terrific heat coming up through the carpet, and then I saw that there was a large crack across the hearthstone.

I knelt down in front of the fire, to observe the cracked hearthstone better, and found I had to get up quickly, because my knees were burning with the heat coming up through the carpet. 'Don't go to work, Ivor,' I said, 'This house is on fire!'

Just as I was saying that, the bus arrived at the door, and Ivor jumped up and ran out. I called after him, 'Don't go, Ivor, don't go! The house is on fire!' But Ivor was now under military orders to work in the colliery and it was an offence to take a shift off work, one liable to be prosecuted by the military authorities. An offender would be treated as a deserter, and Ivor was too anxious not to be accused of this to realise what I was saying.

I locked the door behind my husband, and called the children to me.

'I want you to do exactly as I tell you,' I said. 'And don't ask questions, there's no time. We've got a fire here somewhere. Jack, you and Pearl go in the shop and bring all the boilers that are hanging from the bar on the ceiling—climb on the counter, Jack, and hand them down to Pearl. Then, Pearl, you must take the boilers down to the basement one at a time, and put them by the bathroom.'

(Fortunately I had bought twenty-four tin boilers from the travelling tinkers some days previously. The boilers were good sellers in the shop; they replaced the heavy old iron boilers that women had previously had to lift onto the fire to boil their washing in—these were the days before detergents and washing machines.)

We had no telephone and the nearest kiosk was more than a mile away, so I couldn't call the Fire Brigade, and I had no idea what else to do. Yet I had to do something, I couldn't go to bed and leave things as they were. So I took it to the Lord in prayer, and asked for His guidance and protection in whatever we had to do. Then I went downstairs to the basement and looked up at the ceiling; it was black and bellying down, and when I put the back of my hand against it, I knew that the fire was there. I knew too that there wasn't a minute to lose before that ceiling gave way, and once the air got to the fire, the whole thing would break and there would be no hope of saving the house. It would go up in flames—and we could not possibly risk that with the German bombers going over us. Yet there could be no help from outside, it depended entirely on how we tackled it ourselves.

I gave Jack and Pearl instructions to fill every boiler with cold water from the bath tap while I prepared the room upstairs, then I pulled the table and chairs away from the fireplace down to the bottom end of the room, leaving the fireplace area free. (The room was narrow and fairly long.) Next I helped Jack and Pearl to bring the boilers up to the sitting room (though leaving some of them on the basement stairs), and when that was done, I took the rugs up off the floor and rolled back the carpet, which was badly scorched. In fact it was so dry and burnt that it was breaking as I rolled it up, and I could see that the cork lino had melted. I had no need to take the lino up because I could see the cracks in the floorboards from where the cork had melted.

I took a knife in my hand and said to Jack, 'Stand by me now, with a boiler full of water. As soon as I put this knife down into the crack of the floorboard, a flame will come up. Don't wait to be told, pour the water on it.'

I put the knife down into the crack, as I had said I would, then I jumped back as a big flame singed my hair. Jack poured the whole boiler full of water over it and quickly quenched the flame, but we used the whole twenty-four boilers of water before I was satisfied that there was no more fire left in the ceiling, and to make sure there wasn't even a spark of fire left, I put my hand around the hole. When I got up to survey the damage, I found that more than half of the sitting room floor had fallen through into the basement, as charred powder. There was nothing more we could do that night except go to bed, we were all too exhausted, but we had saved the building.

However, before I got into bed, I knocked at my mother's bedroom door. She and my stepfather were both asleep, and hadn't heard a thing.

'Mam,' I said, 'when you get up in the morning, don't be frightened. I've made an awful mess in your living room in the basement.'

'Oh that's all right,' she replied. 'We'll soon clean it up.'

'No, Mam,' I said, 'you won't be able to clean this. I'm only telling you because we've had a bit of a fire, but it's quite safe now, I didn't want you to be frightened when you get up and see what's happened.'

At half past six the next morning I went downstairs to open the door and let Ivor in.

'Be careful when you go into the sitting room,' I told him, 'because there's a big hole there.'

When he saw the state of the place, the blood drained from his face. 'You had the Fire Brigade?' he asked.

'No, the children and I put it out by ourselves,' I explained.

As the premises were leasehold, I had to report the fire at once to the National Coal Board. Shortly the insurance people arrived to inspect the damage, and they called in the Fire Brigade who came quickly. That said it was the worst "hearth-fire" they had ever seen, and it was evident from the charred wood that it had been smouldering inside for weeks. From the questions they asked and the replies I gave when I told them of the brown ceiling that had bellied down and burnt my hand, they were able to tell the insurance people (who were there listening and taking notes) that if I had not noticed the crack in the hearth and we had gone straight to bed that night, we would have been burnt to death. There would have been no chance of escape, as it was evident from the bellying that the ceiling would have fallen that night, the air would have got in, and flames would have been all through the house in seconds. And all the houses in Tonna Road would have gone up along with it, they said, because they were all so dry. A further added danger was that the bombers going over to Swansea would have seen the fire and dropped their bombs.

The firemen set to work and cleaned all the basement out, so that when my mother came down later in the morning, the place was beautifully clean, although she had no ceiling over her head!—and we had no floor beneath our feet in the sitting room, either! When the insurance men and the Fire Brigade expressed amazement that we had put the blaze out ourselves without showing a chink of light, I told them, 'It was done by the power of prayer.'

Mr. Phillips, head of the N.C.B., said, 'We will put the men on the job of repairing your house without delay.'

'Could I have a better quality grate if I pay the difference?' I asked.

'Yes, you shall have a better quality grate,' he agreed, 'but *we* will pay the difference. What you and your little band of "firemen" did has saved us thousands of pounds, so we will do the best we can for you.'

EIGHTEEN

After all the officials had left, I knew I had another problem. My mother and stepfather were too old to stand the racket the carpenters would make, sawing and banging, and they were too old as well to remain in those living conditions while the work was going on. I would have to find accommodation for them immediately, but where that could be, I had no idea, though I wanted to keep them near to me, as they were afraid of the planes flying overhead.

The day was cold, so I put a coat on and went out in the road. I looked up and down the street and wondered who in all these one hundred and ten three-storey houses would be able or willing to accommodate an old couple—and whether the place would be suitable for them. I stood in silent prayer and asked the all-seeing God to help me find a home nearby for them. My house was number 90, so I started from 91 and listened for our Lord's instructions; I knew He would help me.

As I passed each house, I knew that there would be no accommodation there, until I reached number 103; I would have passed that house too, as it was the home of a young couple who had only recently moved in. The young man was the curate of St. Peter's Church, Nantyfyllon, but as my faith was Baptist, I didn't know him or his wife, and I felt sure that they wouldn't want to let any of their rooms. However I knew that this was the house at which God intended me to call, so I knocked loudly on the door. The young curate answered my knock, and I said, 'Good morning, I have a problem. Can you help me, please?'

I told him about the fire, and my aged parents, and my desire to find them suitable accommodation, then I repeated, 'Can you help me, please, Mr. Thomas?' He readily agreed, saying, 'There's plenty of empty rooms here. Let them come down right away and I will have a nice fire waiting for them. They can have the whole of this ground floor, because my wife and I and our little daughter live in the basement. We haven't furnished all the

120

rooms, as I was hoping to be offered a church of my own, and now we will be leaving the house in the next few weeks and moving to England where I *have* been offered a church. As your parents will be sitting tenants, they will have a chance of the tenancy after us.'

The firemen had not yet left my house, and they carried the furniture down to number 103. My mother and stepfather were comfortably settled there that same morning, so as we had no floor in our sitting room, we were able to move our furniture back into the basement. (Through the floorless sitting room we were able to see when customers came into the shop!)

As the war was getting more serious now, my sister-in-law returned to my home from London; she brought with her her baby, her mother and her ten-year-old niece, and planned to spend the duration of the war with me. We were all able to live together in the large basement flat, and with the sitting room now repaired, we could use that room as a business office.

By now my health was causing great anxiety to my doctor and my husband, and I was ordered to bed. The doctor feared that I would suffer a cardiac arrest, and as there was a special instrument needed to prevent this happening—a special needle to pierce the heart—they sent out an SOS over the air for it. The needle was flown from some country abroad to Cardiff, where an ambulance was waiting to bring it up to Maesteg. Dr. Wishart was waiting for the ambulance in Maesteg, and he brought the needle up to Caerau.

Meanwhile the police had directed the buses to load and unload at points further away from my home, and sawdust was placed thickly on the pavements to deaden any sounds coming from outside the house. My husband's younger sister had come to our house to be with the children. When Dr. Wishart's car pulled up some distance from the house that morning, he took the special instrument and ran across the road, down to the side entrance and into my basement flat, then up the two flights of stairs to my bedroom. My mother and my husband were standing in the bedroom, while Dr. Sinclair bent over my body with a mirror pressed to my mouth. He took it away and when he lifted it up, he found no sign of breath on it. As Dr. Wishart came into the bedroom, Dr. Sinclair raised his hand and said, 'Too late, John, she's gone.'

While this was happening, Mrs. Hurley, an elderly customer of ours, who had seen Dr. Wishart run from his car, was anxious, and followed him down to my living room. She said to my sister-in-law, 'How is Mrs. Webb?' and got the reply, 'Mrs. Webb is dying.' On hearing these words my little daughter Pearl, who was twelve years old then, ran up the two flights of stairs screaming 'Mammy! Mammy!'

As for me, while I lay there, I could see our Lord and Saviour Jesus Christ standing by my bed, arrayed in a beautiful white robe, and stretching out His arms towards me, with a gentle smile on His lovely face. I felt myself rising to go to Him; free at last from pain, I longed to go to those loving arms.

And then my daughters screams penetrated my mind, and I heard my mother's voice say, 'Hush, love.'

Pearl answered, 'I can't hush, Gran, when I know my mammy's dying.' I looked into the face of our Lord and said, 'Please may I stay a little longer? My little ones need me.'

Our Lord's arms dropped slowly down to his sides, and a look of disappointment came over His gentle face. I couldn't bear to see that disappointed look, and my children and my responsibilities to them faded from my memory. I only wanted to see the smile come back to His face, and I called out to Him, 'Not *my* will, dear Lord, but Thine, be done.' The smile came back to His face; He raised His hand in blessing, and disappeared. I began to breathe again, and returned to life, although I didn't regain consciousness for some time.

Some months later I asked Dr. Wishart and Dr. Sinclair if they had seen what I saw on the morning I was asssumed dead. They both said, 'No, Mrs. Webb, we didn't see what *you* saw. But we saw a miracle!'

Slowly I recovered, but it was quite a long time before I was allowed to go down to the room behind the shop. One day when I was sitting there, I could hear children singing a beautiful song, "Cymru Lân" (Lovely Wales), from Tyderwen School opposite and I asked my husband to take me out and leave me at the front door for a while, to listen to the children. Several times recently Lord Haw Haw had called out over the airways, "You people of Maesteg think you are safe, but we're coming to blow up your collieries soon, and your arsenal in Bridgend," and I was thinking of this as I listened. (Every night since the commencement of the war my children and I had prayed, "Please, God, protect our

122

Sergeant-Major Garfield Llewellyn Bowen. Master Gunner, in command of Pen-Lee Fort, Plymouth. (Author's Brother).

This is the house. All that white that looks like rubbish is cabbages.

Young Jimmy with his Daddy.

Jim on the Harvester. I could not get the horses in, there are eight of them.

arsenal in Bridgend and our collieries throughout the valleys from the German bombers.')

Then the children's singing finished, and they were let out to play. The din was terrific. I was looking up towards the playground, hoping to see my little boy Ivan at play, when I noticed, out of the corner of my eye, a huge, black object in the sky, coming towards the school. At first I just watched this moving object out of curiosity, then as it came closer to the school I realised it was a plane, but thought it might be one of ours. Then the thought struck me, "Suppose it's a German plane, and they've come to fire at the little children in the playground?" According to recent news several schools had been machine-gunned during playtime, so I feared for the safety of our little ones, and turned again to God, praying that He would direct the plane away from the school.

I was still watching the plane, and I saw it disappear behind the school, and reappear, as if it was going towards Dyffryn Woods. Then I saw a parcel drop from the plane, and then another one and another one, and as they came nearer to the ground what looked like large umbrellas opened out from them, turning them slightly on their sides and filling them with the wind coming up the valley. A man was hanging from each umbrella, and they were blowing towards the woods, over the Cymmer mountains.

The sound of the plane had been drowned by the noise of the children in the playground, and it was now disappearing over the Cymmer mountains. The time was past eleven o'clock in the morning and the streets were deserted. The colliers were either at work in the colliery or in bed after their night shift, and the women and girls were all working down in the arsenal in Bridgend. Then three young teenage boys appeared on the scene, and I told them to go quickly to the police station in Caerau, as I had seen an aeroplane drop three parachutists. The boys only laughed, thinking I was joking, and went on their way. I was very worried, but I couldn't go into the house to call to anyone for help, because I was unable to walk.

Then I saw a council worker whom I knew coming down the road, and I called out to him, 'Mr. Isaac, will you call the police, please?' I repeated to him what I had already told the boys, but Mr. Isaac came towards me and said, 'Go in and lie down, bach, you've been very ill.' Then *he* went on his way.

I was frantic, and didn't know what to do, when a woman came

123

out of a house higher up the street. Her father, Mr. Waters, was the head of the Home Guard, so I called to her, 'Fetch your father quick, Mary,' and told her what I'd seen. She went into the house at once, but came out again, shaking her head. 'My father says you've been very ill,' she said, then she too went on her way.

I was desperate now. 'Oh God,' I prayed, 'send somebody quickly, Lord, who will believe me about what I've seen!' Then a little van came down the road from Caerau. I recognized it as the van belonging to a special constable who was also a butcher; he was delivering meat to one of his customers in the street. As he was getting out of his van, I called to him: 'Fred—am I insane?'

'Good God, Mrs. Webb, not you!' he replied.

So I said, 'Well, will you believe me if I tell you something that no-one else will believe?'

'I will indeed, Mrs. Webb. What is it you've seen?' he asked.

I told him the story, and he threw the meat back into the van and held up his fingers, saying, 'Give me three minutes.' Then he turned the van around and headed back the way he had come, towards the police station.

Next thing the valley was aroused by all the sirens from the collieries and the fire station screaming out their message, and in seconds the men of the Home Guard were running from all directions to Mr. Waters's house to report for orders. Then Mr. Waters, with his tin helmet on and his gasmask strapped over his shoulder, came down with the rest of his men, and asked me what had happened. 'What have you seen, Mrs. Webb?' he enquired.

By now I was exhausted, and some of the Home Guard carried me back into my sitting room. I told Mr. Waters, '*You* didn't believe me. I'll tell the police when they come.' At that a loud voice boomed out; it was Police Sergeant Bloomer.

'Here I am, Mrs. Webb,' he said. 'Tell me what you've seen.'

I told him, and he asked me in what direction the plane had gone and where it had dropped the men. At that, I told him it had come up the valley behind the school, dropped the men over Tonna David Farm, and then made its way over towards the Afan valley. Within minutes people were watching the Home Guard climbing all over the mountains in the direction the plane had taken. The day wore on, and at four o'clock those men due on the night shift returned home, and the day shift Home Guard men took over from them. People called out, 'Did you find them?' but the men replied, 'No sign of them.'

124

I prayed, "Please, God, let them find those men or they'll be taking me to a mental hospital!" I had visions of becoming a mental patient. Nothing was heard until Sergeant Bloomer came down at seven o'clock in the evening to tell me that the three had been captured. 'One was caught hiding in the ferns, making a sketch plan of Caerau Colliery. He already had the plans of St. John's Colliery, Maesteg, and Coegnant Colliery, Caerau, on his person. And the other two men were captured with the plans of the collieries in the Afan Valley.'

The sergeant said that if they hadn't caught the men before nightfall, they would have radioed all the information back to their base, and Lord Haw Haw would have had the satisfaction of seeing all the collieries in the Afan and Llynfi valleys blown to atoms.

I could only attribute this deliverance to the power of the prayers of thousands of ordinary people, praying for the safety of their collieries and their valleys. And God had given me the privilege of serving Him when He brought me back from death and put me on my doorstep in time to see that plane and report it to the police. (And, of course, the Llynfi valleys owed much, as did every part of Britain, to the hard work and devotion to their country, of the Home Guard.)

On the following Monday Mr. Diamond, my traveller, called in from Bridgend. He was very excited when he came into the shop, and he said to my husband, 'Hey! What do you think of Caerau now! It's really on the map!'

'What do you mean, Charlie?' asked Ivor. 'On the map?'

'Well,' he said, 'haven't you heard? You've got a smart woman up here in Caerau who saw three Germans come down by parachute. It's all over Bridgend—that's all everybody's talking about—and you in Caerau haven't heard!'

Ivor laughed, and said, 'Here's your "smart woman"—my wife!'

'You, Mrs. Webb?' said Charlie. 'I didn't know you were out of bed, you were so ill for so long.'

'Yes,' I agreed. 'That's why the Germans nearly got away, because no-one would believe me—they thought it was my imagination until Fred Bennett came along and called the police for me.'

Charlie was so excited; he said, 'Wait till I go to Bridgend and tell them down there that it was my customer in Caerau who caught them!'

Indeed, such was his excitement that he ran out of the shop, jumped into his car, and didn't realize until he got to Bridgend that he hadn't collected our money or taken our order! He had to turn around and come all the way back.

NINETEEN

Now at last I was able to look around my shop, and I was shocked to see all the shelves practically empty. Although I'd been ill, and confined to my bedroom for six months, I remembered the shop being packed with goods on display, and I knew that if the shop had been run as efficiently as it had been when I was there, it would still be well stocked. When Ivor came down from his bed that day, I asked him what had happened to the shop.

'What have you done with all the stock we had?' I said. 'Where are all the boxes we piled up on each step of the stairs—and all the cases of tinned goods packed in the cellar?'

(I had already had a chance to see that though my two sisters-in-law had been helping to look after the shop while I was ill, they didn't have the same experience or knowledge of the business that I did, and though our customers got their rations at the weekend, there was not sufficient of the unrationed goods to satisfy their needs.)

Ivor looked ill and sick with worry. 'Don't ask me, Ray,' he said. 'I don't know what is going on here. I go to work every night on the bus at nine o'clock, then I come home at half-past six in the morning, and after I have my bath I have to get as much sleep as possible or I would not be fit for the next night shift. And they get upset downstairs if I as much as show myself in the shop, and tell me. "There's no need for you to come in here; we can look after it." '

One sister-in-law, with her mother and two children, had come as an evacuee family; there were four of them, and the government paid just ten shillings per week for each of the two children. Otherwise no money passed, and my sister-in-law had offered to care for the home and the shop in lieu of payment for herself and her mother; my husband's sister had also offered her services. Both meant well, but their lack of experience left us with many problems, and my own children had had to work much harder than I would have allowed them to do.

Ivor told me, 'I take every Friday off from work, as you

127

know, Ray, and I'm risking prosecution by the government just to make sure that everybody gets their fair share of rationed goods, but what else happens to the foodstuffs throughout the week, God only knows—I don't.'

'Well, there'll be no more worry for you,' I told him. 'I'm taking over now.'

'You're not fit to be in the shop, Ray,' he said. 'You can't stand, you're too weak.'

'With God's help, I'll make myself strong,' I said. 'My children shall no longer work like drudges, and we'll build up the shop again.'

I thanked the one sister-in-law for her help, and said, 'There will be no need for you to put yourself to further trouble on our behalf. I'm taking over again.'

Then, to the evacuees I said, 'I'll relieve you of the burden of looking after the shop now. I've had a long enough rest and I'm taking over now. I must sort out the business again, because from what I see of my books, there's a lot of debt owing.'

I had a number of travellers who had supplied me since 1935 when I started in business, and I had never owed anything to anyone, but now they all had huge outstanding accounts. When the wholesalers came to the shop, I asked them why there was all this debt outstanding, and they replied, 'Your sisters-in-law always told us that they couldn't pay the bills, Mr. Webb was in bed, and Mrs. Webb was too ill to be bothered. We continued to supply goods to you because of our past dealings with you—we know that when you were well enough to take over the business yourself, all this would be settled.' My two helpers had not understood the importance of not letting bills accumulate, and it took two years of hard going before these debts were all cleared.

One day, to add to our anxieties, my husband was called to appear at a police court on the charge of being absent from work on one day every week over a period of several months. This worried us greatly, as it was a very serious charge and we knew what the consequences might be. They day of the police court hearing arrived, and Ivor had to attend. Being unused to court proceedings, he went alone, but he had told Dr. Wishart of the hearing and to his surprise, he saw the doctor in court. Dr. Wishart asked permission to speak for my husband, and told them of my illness, explaining the case to them.

Then the Clerk of the Court got up and spoke, again in Ivor's favour, saying, 'We have brought this man here to condemn him for losing one shift a week, although he has furnished the colliery each week with a medical certificate stating that his wife has been suffering from an advanced heart condition and was confined to her bed for six months. Not only that, the man is suffering from stone dust in the lungs, but he answered the call of duty and went back to the colliery for his country's sake. By night he works in the colliery, by day he cares for his sick wife and three children, and he also has his wife's business to run. He takes a Friday night off, so that he can have one night's rest a week. Instead of condemning this man, we should be applauding him! Is there any man in this court who, if similarly placed, could do more? I myself could not do as much.'

Then the judge said to my husband, 'Mr. Webb, you are indeed a good man, and should never have been brought to this court. I haven't the authority to tell you to stay home from work, but I do have the authority to tell you to go only when you can. Case dismissed.' After that, life went on quietly, and the shop began to fill with off-the-ration goods again; slowly but surely my debts were getting less, thanks to the patience of all my suppliers.

One very wet day, when I had a few customers in the shop, the sirens went. The customers had to leave their goods on the counter and run back to the safety of their own homes, while I went out to my shop door to turn the key in the lock until the "All Clear" sounded. As I did so, I heard a lot of distressed children crying and I went out through the door to see what was the matter. Cars were dashing up and down the road in a hurry to get to safety, but I could see that about fifty yards down the street, where the school gate opened on to the pavement, there was a large crowd of children, many of them infants, crying because they couldn't cross the road to get to their homes, owing to the speed of the traffic.

The children had all been trained in school to leave their classrooms quickly and quietly immediately they heard the siren, and proceed, all of them, down to the bottom of the playground; they were to do this as orderly as possible, without panic, and with some of the teachers to see them safely off the premises. Infants and girls were to proceed quickly down one steep flight of stone steps to the main gate, and the boys were to go down the opposite flight of steps to the main gate.

Many of the children lived in Tonna Road, but the majority of them lived across the valley, about half a mile away. These children had to cross the main road and go down a steep rough lane that went past my shop and around the back of the premises. Then they went down another lane, between fields, to the river, which they had to cross by a little wooden bridge, not much more than planks across the water (in rough weather these would be awash). Next they went up another lane to another main road which they would have to cross to get to their own streets. The children were taught that the moment the sirens sounded, they had to start that long journey, but they were given only three minutes—just the time during which the sirens were still screaming—to reach the safety of their homes; this was under threat of punishment if they were still on the road after the stipulated time, when the sirens stopped.

Now these rain-soaked children were standing, crying, on the pavement. The teachers were safely back inside the school, and any child attempting to cross the road could have been injured or killed. I saw their predicament, and ran down through the middle of the street, holding out my arms to stop the traffic. I was wearing my white shop coat—there had been no time to put on a mac, or put anything on my head. I stood in the middle of the road and held out my arms to halt the traffic both ways, then I called to the children, 'Come along, cross now,' which they did, reaching safety on the other side.

The drivers pulled down their windows and shouted abuse at me, many of them using strong language, but I replied, 'These children have to reach safety, and if you're afraid, park your cars on the sides of the road and shelter in any of these houses. If you are such cowards that you can't see the dangers for these little children, then you should be where their fathers and brothers are, in the firing line, fighting for men like you.'

I had my say before I let the cars go, but they still reported me to the police for obstructing them. However from that day on it became my custom, whenever the siren sounded during school hours, to empty my shop immediately and run to bring the children safely across the road, always wearing my white shop coat. This went on for some months before the police decided they would have to investigate the complaints. One day, while I was guiding the children across the road, Sergeant Bloomer and one of his police officers arrived on the scene. They stopped and watched me bring the children across the road, with all the cars held back on the side, and Sergeant Bloomer said, 'So it's you, Mrs. Webb, causing all these complaints!' He looked serious, but then he burst into laughter and said, 'Well done!' And from that the "lollipop man/woman" had its birth.

Some weeks later the sergeant came to the shop and asked me if I would take my "escort duty" on as a regular and permanent job; I would have to direct the children across the road, to and from school, in the morning, at midday, and in the evening, for a payment of thirty shillings (£1.50) per week. I told the sergeant that I only did it for the safety of the children during air raids, and I would continue to do that, but only for the children's safety, not for payment. I couldn't take it on as a paid job because I had my business and my family to look after. So then the sergeant asked if my husband would take on the job.

I called Ivor to the shop, but he told Sergeant Bloomer, 'I work nights in the colliery, I can't be on the road all day. Sometimes I go out during an air raid in place of my wife, because she is not always well enough to run. But covering the crossing is not all she does. She has turned our downstairs living room into a First Aid room for the little children. The infants are too small, and can't possibly reach their homes at the other side of the valley in three minutes. My side entrance is as far as they can go before the warning sirens stop, so it's their custom now to come in through there, and we care for them at our house during the raids. These are all very frightened little ones, and many of them wet themselves with fear. Others fall and are cut and scratched by the roughness of the lane. My wife cares for their wounds, bathing and bandaging them, and dries their wet clothes, then with toys we try to take away their fear until the "All Clear goes. Then we see them safely back to school.'

The sergeant said, 'We have two other schools in Caerau which have dangerous crossings near them, and we have a lot of injured children. What you have done at Tyderwen School has been brought to the notice of the Glamorgan Constabulary, and a meeting was held to decide that we would use your methods outside the other two schools to see if we could cut down on child injuries. Can you recommend any suitable people for this work?'

My husband said, 'It's a very good idea, and many people who are unfit for military service would be glad of the extra money. In the meantime, my wife and I will look after these children. I'll

131

see them safely to school, in the morning before I go to bed, and at four o'clock in the evening when they are coming out of school, and my wife will see to them during the dinner hour and during air raids. But we won't accept payment, that would be too binding. And we'll do this until you can find someone suitable, but please get someone as soon as you can because we are both overworked as it is, and have more than enough to do.'

We manned that road for more than a year, but as far as we could see, the police made no effort to put anyone in our place. So my husband took it on himself to interview some suitable women, and chose Mrs. Olive Owen, of Number 4, Tonna Road. He sent her up to the police station to be signed on and fitted out with a suitable white coat and hat, and then, with police authority, she started her new job at once. She was a faithful lollipop woman for fifteen years, until one morning during the August school holidays she was found dead in bed. She had been planning to go for a caravanning holiday in Porthcawl.

One day some councillors came to my shop, asking me for my vote. One of the councillors was the headmaster of Nantyfyllon School, while the candidate himself was a well-known solicitor from the valley.

I said to them, 'While I am making up my mind as to who shall have our vote, will you come for a little walk with me? I have something to show you.' I called Jack in to look after the shop, while I went with the men, and then I took them down the lane, pointing out the state of the pathway, rough and broken so that it caused injuries for far too many of the little children. Next I showed them what passed for a bridge, just a little wooden platform crossing the river, wet and slippery, with broken sides. Often it was awash with river water.

I told them that this was a disgrace to any valley, and I wondered that many children had not been washed off that bridge into the river and drowned. 'That could still happen, you know,' I said, 'especially when the river is in flood. More than a hundred children travel up and down this way every day, and all of them are under the age of eleven. Now, the man who'll get my vote—and the votes of all the mothers and fathers of these children—will be the one who will promise to put a solid bridge here, and resurface the lane, making it fit for them to travel.'

The men said it would cost a tremendous amount of money to tarmac the whole lane, at which I told them that I knew how they could do it quite cheaply. 'The Council will be resurfacing the road shortly, so I've been told. You can have all that old tarmac brought down and used to surface this lane. Then all you'll need will be a little manpower and a roller. There's plenty of men in Tonna Road who will gladly give you the manpower—free.'

They promised that the work should be done, and later on it was, just as I had suggested. A nice, solid bridge was put over the river, and the lane was tarmacked.

TWENTY

Several times a week fresh leaflets, in sealed envelopes marked "Private and Confidential", were put in through our letterbox. These were instructions from the government, which all shopkeepers were supposed to read, memorise and destroy. For example, we were told what to do in the event of the invasion of our valley by the enemy. Shopkeepers were ordered to open their doors, and they were to be cheerful and give confidence to their customers. On no account must a shopkeeper show fear or evacuate his or her premises, because that could start a panic, and people fleeing from danger would obstruct the roads and prevent heavy military transport from using them; that would help the enemy, and we must not do that at any cost.

Also we were told that should a strange man come to our door at any time during the day or night, we should make him feel welcome, but if we had any suspicion of him, we should ask him in for a cup of tea and ask him to say these words: "Wendell Wilkie". Should he pronounce the words "Vendell Vilkie", we would know that he was a German, and we should try to keep him there, without arousing his suspicions, until we could contact the police, who would come and take him away.

In our shop we had large posters warning people that careless talk was dangerous. People were not supposed to discuss anything concerning the war while they were waiting to be served or standing around in groups talking, because you never knew who might be listening and careless words could lose us the war. Street names were obliterated or taken down, the signposts were removed or painted over. Each street and corner was known to the police by number, not by name, and every policeman had to memorize all these numbers. Any car could be confiscated at any time for military purposes, or for police use in connection with the military.

Another source of great anxiety for shopkeepers, in addition to the extra work caused by rationing and the fact that food had to

134

be cut up into small pieces with great accuracy, was the Inspectorate of Food Control. These inspectors would invade our shops at the most unexpected times, particularly when you were at your busiest, cutting up the rations.

One Friday morning I was in my shop, which was full of customers all waiting to be served, when two men, looking very stern and wearing an air of great importance, stepped inside the door. One man stood outside the counter, with his back to the door, as if to stop anyone from going out, while the other one, without so much as a word, pushed past the customers, lifted the flap of the counter, and walked past me without even an "excuse me".

He went straight to the scales, which he examined minutely, looking underneath to see that nothing had been attached to the scales that could cause loss of weight to the customer and gain to the shopkeeper. Having done that, he crossed around to the other side of the shop and examined the sweet scales, while the other man watched that no-one behind the counter interfered with these scales before the inspector could examine them. Then the inspector inside the counter asked me to show him the vegetable scales, which I did.

'Your scales are in good order, Mrs. Webb, and well maintained,' he said.

'Yes, I pay maintenance on them all,' I told him.

Then he went to a box of groceries on the counter; they had been put up ready for collection by one of our customers. He took every item out of the box, weighed everything and checked the weight against the ration books and the bill put in with the groceries. At last, very grudgingly, he grunted, 'Hmm. Everything all right there,' as if he was disappointed that he hadn't caught me out in some dishonest action. Then he stood behind me, watching me as I served the customers and weighed out their rations. It was very nerve-racking. Although I had nothing to fear as regards my honesty in dealing with my customers, his presence made me nervous because I might easily make an honest mistake. The hostility in the looks and the voices of these inspectors made the shopkeepers feel embarrassed in front of their customers, and they would stay for so long that it hindered the smooth running of a shop, especially when children came in with their sweet coupons and you had to cut out their tiny coupons, minute, but essential to your business because without them you could not replenish your stock.

135

One Thursday, when the war had been on for several years, and this embarrassment with the inspectors was happening roughly about once every month to six weeks, I was down in the basement, taking advantage of a little quiet in the shop to rest for a while. The shop bell rang, and my thirteen-year-old daugher, Pearl, went up to the shop. I got up to follow her, and overheard her saying, with much scorn and emphasizing her words, 'Oh, it's you horrible men again, is it?'

One man answered, quite nicely, 'Oh, we're horrible men, are we? Why?'

'Yes, you are horrible,' she said. 'You come to this shop and you upset my mother and make her ill. My mother is honest, and everyone knows that!'

She was very upset and tearful, so they said, 'All right, my dear, we won't upset her today.' They walked out, and I never saw them again.

Ivan, my younger boy, was now a pupil at the Preparatory School in Bridgend, and he was having voice-training lessons with a Mr. Watkins, in Garth, which is a mile outside Maesteg. Twice a week I had to take him down in the evening for his voice-training, and we would usually take the local bus down to Maesteg, and then walk the remainder of the way—or if we were lucky, we'd have a bus ride. Mr. Watkins, who was a bachelor, lived with his sister and brother-in-law, who were bakers and pastry-cooks; the sister, Maud Bowen, was a friend of mine of many years' standing. The Bowens had an only son, Henry, a year older than Ivan, and also a pupil at the Preparatory School in Bridgend. While Ivan was having his lesson, I would be in the living room, having a cup of tea with Maud.

After the lesson Henry would usually take Ivan down to show him his pony in the field, and between the two of them they would often cause me to lose the last bus up to Caerau. Then Ivan and I would have to walk all the way home, about three miles in the blackout, which was no mean task, as there would not be a glimmer of light anywhere. It was difficult to find your way home in the pitch dark. If there was no traffic about, we would walk on the main road, because there we would make better progress, not having to watch out for the kerbs on the pavement, but we would continually be bumping into other pedestrians who were walking in the opposite direction, to whom we had to say "sorry". It was

136

always a relief when we arrived home safely, though our only fear was of falling over pavements and doorsteps. Often when we reached home, my shoulders and arms would be bruised through bumping into the walls of houses and falling over gutters. But that was life in wartime, and we were lucky if we got home without an air raid warning, because if there was a warning, the wardens patrolling the streets could order you to take shelter.

One day, at the beginning of the war, an advertisement had appeared in the paper asking for families who were willing to give free hospitality to serving men in the Forces, to register with Lady Frances Rider and Miss Fry. I was very willing to give free hospitality to either British or Dominion soliders, so I wrote off, and received a form which had to be signed by three professional people who would verify my honesty and my ability to provide and care for these men. The hostesses were required to be married, with two or three children; they must have a piano in their house for entertainment, must be sober, and must not allow gambling in the house. I could meet all these requirements, and my form was signed by my bank manager, the minister of my church, and a member of the police force.

Lady Frances Rider and Miss Fry thanked me for my application, and said they would be pleased to send someone down to me when the scheme started, which would be in the near future. It was 1940 and the Battle of Britain was raging. One morning my sister-in-law, who usually got up early to wash and dress her baby, got up rather earlier than usual, almost as if she knew that something unexpected was going to happen! I was an early riser too, because my children had to catch the early bus to get to their schools in Bridgend, but that morning Evelyn knocked at my bedroom door before I was up, and said, 'Come down, Rit, I've got a shock for you down there. You've got ten extra people for breakfast!'

I put on my dressing gown and slippers, and hurried downstairs to see who these ten people could be. They were a pitiful sight—some were elderly men and women, and some younger mothers (though they had no children with them); their homes had been destroyed by bombs and they themselves had been dug out from amongst dead bodies in the air raid shelters near their homes. They were dirty and bloody, and their hastily applied bandages were also soiled with muck and blood. They said that they had been given my address by Evelyn's sister (whose little daughter Patsy was also one of my evacuees). It seemed that anyone in distress who knew an address in Wales could go to the railway station, produce the address, and be given a free railway warrant to take them to the place named. Hence they had all used this one address, hoping I would give them shelter, because they had nowhere else to go.

Evelyn said she didn't know any of them, but I couldn't see them left out on the road, so we set to and made breakfast for them all. Then they took it in turns to clean themselves up in the bathroom, and we applied fresh bandages to their injuries. Luckily there were no broken bones, but I had to take many of them to the surgery later in the day, for medical attention. Bread was rationed, and this made feeding them a little difficult, but fortunately I had plenty of margarine and sugar (supplied for my ice-cream allocation) and I could use some of that for them until I could get supplementary ration cards for them.

After breakfast, while my visitors were taking it in turns to clean themselves in the bathroom, I called my younger children down to the sitting room and prepared them there for school—there was no room to see to them in the basement as I usually did. The schools my children attended were Bridgend schools, but because the air raid shelters at the schools were not adequate, they travelled backwards and forwards as day pupils. Their dinners were included in their school fees, so I didn't have to cut lunches for them (which was fortunate that day, as our "guests" had eaten all our bread!)

When the children were dressed, ready for school, we had our inspection parade. They had to show their wrists for me to see that their identity discs were secure; the discs were silver bands with the child's name, address and registration number engraved on each one. Pearl's registration number was XJOF 607 4, and Ivan's, XJOF 706 5. After that I asked, 'Have you got your identity card in your pocket? Clean handkerchief and pocket money? Gas mask?' The gas mask was inside a cylinder, hanging by a cord over the child's one shoulder, while the school bag hung over the other shoulder. When I was satisfied that they had everything they were required by law to carry, I saw them safely off on the bus.

Jack was still taking private tuition in engineering, in preparation for starting an apprenticeship with Shepherd and

Sons in Bridgend, but in between his lessons he helped me in the shop. That morning I left him in charge and went down to the offices of the Ministry of Food in Maesteg, where I told them that these people were not in a fit condition to come down themselves, but anyone who wanted could come up and confirm that I needed ten supplementary ration papers. They gave the papers to me, and I was back in time to get rations of bread etc for the visitors, but I had to do it at my own expense, because they had no money.

I knew that I couldn't keep my "guests" with me, I would have to go out in the afternoon to look for lodgings for them, and depend on the kindness of people to get them taken in as evacuees. The government would then pay for their keep—ten shillings a week per person. (This was because they had been bombed out; adults like my sister-in-law and her mother, who had not lost their homes, did not receive any payment.) Evelyn and her mother, Mrs. Hall, were kept busy all morning, preparing the vegetables for dinner, since there were now nineteen people to cook for, while I walked the streets all afternoon, till my feet were tired, trying to persuade people to take in some of the evacuees; I was lucky enough to get some who agreed to do so—though they would take only one.

The next morning my sister-in-law came to my bedroom door and said, 'I've got another shock for you. We've got seventeen this time!' And the morning after that another twenty-four arrived, and then more again, so that in the course of one week I had been sent over a hundred people to shelter, all of them bombed out of their homes, and often dug out of collapsed air raid shelters. They had lost everything they possessed, and didn't even have the price of a meal ticket on them. I was at my wits' end, but I couldn't see them left out on the streets. I thought perhaps the Council would do something to help, as they knew all these people were coming to me, but they apparently thought it a great joke, and named my home "The Halfway House".

At last I took the law into my own hands and looked around for places that I could confiscate—with or without permission! I found a large house (called "Llynfi House") behind the police station in Caerau; it was empty and in beautiful condition, and it could accommodate four families. Next I went to the Council and told them that I wanted beds, blankets and furniture, as I was rehousing four families; no-one offered any opposition to my "confiscating" Llynfi House and I already had the key in my

139

possession. (As the evacuees didn't want to be separated, I had left them all in the house, waiting for furniture to arrive.) The Council officials told me that all they had were army bunk beds and blankets, but I could have as many of these as I wanted, and they would have them delivered to Llynfi House. Happily my old friend Mr. Lockyer, "the Father of Maesteg", came to my aid at this point and furnished the entire house with old stock furniture in excellent condition. When I thanked him for this furniture, he said, 'Oh, it's a bit out of date, and you are welcome.'

I found one or two other premises where I could make use of the bunk beds, then the Council provided all the bedding and dishes, everything for the comfort of the people, and delivered them to the addresses I gave. But still people kept coming and I needed more property again. The "Mission Chapel" in Caerau had a big lower ground floor underneath the church, and I knew that this was empty, and used only for children's tea parties, so I went to see a councillor in Humphries Terrace who I thought could help, and asked if he could give me the key. I told him I was confiscating the property for housing for the newest evacuees, many of whom had now brought their children with them.

'You'll be lucky, Mrs. Webb,' he said. 'I've been trying to get that place for months, for my family in London, and if I can't get it, I'm sure you won't.'

'That's all right,' I told him. 'I've already confiscated the property and I'll get a key from somewhere!'

In fact, the pastor of the mission gave me the key, and wished me the best of luck, but he asked me if I would help him by asking the evacuees who moved in if they would be so kind as not to damage the apple trees in the large garden attached to the building. I promised that I would tell them not to damage either the trees or the garden—and I prayed to God that this would be the last lot of people that would have need to come to my house for shelter. My home, once so immaculate, was showing the strain of housing all these people, and it would take a long time to get it back into its former state. And not only that, though I had given temporary shelter to more than a hundred people, I had not received a penny from the Council or from anyone else, to help me provide food for them.

The four families in Llynfi House caused a lot of anxiety for the police in Caerau. The men were always drinking; they had fights in the house which resulted in broken windows and broken

140

furniture, and then the police would be called in to settle their differences. As for those in the mission house, they didn't stop their children damaging the fruit trees, though they had promised me faithfully that they would, so they were no better than the others. However, there *was* one thing I was grateful for—that they didn't come to my shop, and I didn't see anything of them after I had rehoused them. All these people had seemed so grateful for the shelter and the welcome when they came to my house, as well as for all that the Council and Mr. Lockyer did for them, but they later became very ungrateful; Caerau sighed with relief when the war ended and these people returned to their own homes. My sister-in-law apologised for them, and said that they were a very rough crowd and her sister should never have given my address to them.

TWENTY ONE

Throughout all the problems with the evacuees I had been grateful that my mother and stepfather were comfortably settled in their own home. When Mr. Thomas left to become vicar of his own parish in Newcastle, I went to see the owner of the house (who lived in Garth, Maesteg), and asked if my mother could have the tenancy. The owner said that she knew my mother was a sub-tenant, but she had intended to put her grandson and his wife and children in one part of the house. However, there were only three bedrooms there, and I knew that a family with young children would not agree happily with two old folk. My parents would be the ones to suffer.

I told the owner this, and said that in the interests of my parents, I was willing to pay whatever price they asked as key money, as long as my mother could have the tenancy in her own name. (I guessed that the owner and her family would be happy if they had this key money, but they didn't like to ask for it.) So everybody was happy, and the house was my mother's.

All the strain of the last year or so was telling on my health again, and I had to send my washing and ironing out to a woman in the street, as I didn't feel well enough to cope with all I had to do. One day, when Mrs. Lewis was bringing the washed and ironed clothes back to the house, she said, 'Your mother's very worried about you, Mrs. Webb, and she told me to ask you, are you pregnant?'

'Good gracious no, Mrs. Lewis,' I said. 'To the best of my knowledge I am not.'

'Well, to satisfy your mother, I'll go with you to see Dr. Sinclair,' she suggested. So the next morning we went to Dr. Sinclair's surgery in Maesteg. (Dr. Wishart, whose surgery was in Caerau, and who was Dr. Sinclair's partner, had joined the Air Force, and I wanted to speak to Dr. Sinclair himself.) I told the doctor of my mother's fear that I was pregnant, and he said, 'I sincerely hope not. Because if you are, we will have to terminate the pregnancy.'

'I feel sure I'm not,' I told him, 'but if I am, I will be very happy to have the baby.'

'Come and see me in a month's time,' the doctor said, 'and if you are pregnant, I cannot allow you to go through with it. But I will have to have the magistrates' consent to operate.' (Because, of course, it was not legal then to terminate a pregnancy except on the most serious grounds of a medical risk to life.)

'But I don't want to lose it, doctor,' I said. 'It's what I've wanted for years—another child. Why can't I keep it?'

'If you live to carry it,' said Dr. Sinclair, 'You'll never live to give it birth.'

A month to the day I went down to see him again and he said, 'I've had the magistrates' consent, and we will be operating on you tomorrow, so go home and get your things straight away. We can operate on you at this point because we won't have to use chloroform. Your health won't allow you to take chloroform, so we can't risk waiting.'

I went into hospital that day, and the next morning I was prepared for the operation. I had white stockings put on me, and a white gown, and my hair was tied up with a white cloth, as was the custom for an operation. Then I had to wait for the surgeon's signal that I was to be brought down on a stretcher; but while I was waiting, I was very cold and I asked the nurse to give me my dressing gown. I wrapped it round my shoulders but I was still cold, so I said, 'Nurse, give me an eiderdown,' and I wrapped that too around myself; it was the eiderdown off one of my children's beds, but that didn't seem strange, and I still couldn't get warm. Next the trolley came up, with an attendant and a nurse, who went to lift me on to it. 'I'm sorry my bed is so untidy,' I told them, 'but I've been very cold. Take care of the eiderdown, it belongs to my children's beds.'

They put me back into bed, pulled the clothes around me, and closed the curtains. The trolley was pulled away, and the sister sent the nurses round every bed in both the female and male wards to collect all the hot water bottles, fill them with hot water, and bring them quickly to my bed, where they were all packed round my body. I knew nothing of this until later, being semi-conscious at best, but after a while I opened my eyes to see that I was screened from view, and at one side of my bed were Dr. Sinclair and a specialist, while on the other side was my mother, in her apron and carpet slippers.

143

I said, 'Mam, what are you doing here?'

'I was taking a walk down the road,' she said, 'and thought I'd pop in and ask how you were.'

My mother's home was a mile and a half away, and the snow was deep on the ground, yet she said she was out for a walk! Actually she had been brought down hurriedly by the doctor, because it seemed I was dying of a heart attack. (I understood later that the eiderdown and the dressing gown had not been put on my bed; I had seen them in my delirium!) I knew no more until I woke up again some time later to see the sister and Dr. Sinclair bending over me. My mother was not there this time. I asked if the operation was over, and Dr. Sinclair said, 'No, Mrs. Webb, we haven't done the operation. That little old ticker of yours wouldn't let us. You need a long rest, so we are going to put you in a room of your own for six weeks, to give that ticker a chance to recover.'

After six weeks of rest I returned home, without having the operation to terminate my pregnancy, which was now too far advanced for that.

One day I had a telegram from London, saying "Expect eight; four adults and four children." A few hours later a car drew up at my door, bringing my youngest sister, Violet, and her husband and their two children, aged ten and eleven, together with a neighbour of theirs and his wife and *their* two children (of about the same age as Violet's two). I was devastated. I didn't know what to do or where to put them to sleep, but I couldn't refuse them a shelter. I had a number of new eiderdowns in the drapery department of my shop, and I took them all upstairs. There were two single beds in the back bedroom of the house, one Ivan's and the other Jack's, and I put these one at each end of the bedroom, leaving the centre of the floor free to make a bed for the extra children. Next I placed the double-sized bed eiderdowns, one on top of another, on the carpeted floor, making a nice soft bed, and covered them with two large sheets, one over the eiderdowns to protect them from being soiled, and the other to cover the children. Then blankets went on top, to keep the children warm.

I told my sister that she and her husband would have to manage to sleep together in one single bed, while the other man and woman would have to manage in the other bed, while the four

144

children slept on the "floor bed" because there were only three bedrooms in the house.

'As Ivor is working nights,' I explained to them, 'Ivan and Pearl can sleep with me in my bed, but Jack is a teenager and must have a bed to himself, so he can have the small room. I have done the best I can for you, and at least you will have beds and be safe from the bombs until you can find something better.'

They said that they would manage, it was lovely and they were very grateful. Violet called me aside and said, 'Don't worry, Ritt, our friends have got plenty of money. That was their car we came down in; they can afford to put up at a hotel, and they won't stay long.'

A fortnight went by, and our "guests" hadn't even offered to buy a loaf of bread, they just accepted everything as their due. They hadn't attempted to find other accommodation, and it seemed that Violet's friends had settled in with us for good. Unfortunately the visitors' children were unruly too, and they were absolutely ruining my home. They thought nothing of playing "hide and seek" on my furniture—jumping from one settee to another, with no care for the damage they were doing, particularly to my sitting room, which was the room they selected for their boisterous games. In the early hours of the morning the four children would go downstairs and make tea for their parents and themselves, and as they preferred tinned milk in their tea, they would go into my shop and take a tin of sweetened milk, regardless of the fact that this was one of the goods on ration.

Numerous cups of tea were carried up and down the stairs, regardless of the damage to my carpets. In years gone by, in the mining valleys, people's stairs were usually bare, scrubbed boards, and people took pride in keeping them snowy white. Then came the linoleum fashion; the sides of the stairs would be painted, and the lino, which would be about fourteen inches in width, with a plain or mottled pattern and a plain border down each side, would be run down the centre of the stairs. Brown paint was fashionable down the sides, as it was easy to keep clean, sometimes very necessary because of the coal dust that was in the air, due to the collieries.

As pit-head baths had not been thought of in those days, the miners came home in their pit clothes, just as they came from the pit. Their faces would be so black with coal-dust that you could scarcely tell one man from another except by their eyes, which sparkled through the dust, and their lips, which were so red in contrast with their black faces. When I saw them coming down the street in their groups from work, looking and sounding like a lot of blackbirds as they whistled or sang, I felt very proud to be the wife of a miner. They seemed so happy and carefree after coming out of the bowels of the earth, where they'd put in nine or ten hours of hard slogging, that I thought they were like birds who had escaped from their cage, and they seemed so manly, even in the blackness of the coal.

When they got home, the men would have to bathe in front of the fire, in a tin bath, first bending over the bath to wash their top half in the water, which their wives would have heated over an open fire in a boiler. Many of the miners believed that they must not wash their backs more than once a week, or it would make the back too weak for the bending they had to do underground in the colliery. Thus on washing day the wives found it necessary to wash and then to boil the men's vests in an iron or tin boiler over an open fire, with a handful of strong soda added, in order to rub out the dirt that had come off the men's backs. As they took their clothes off, the dry dust from the men would fly through the air and settle over the furniture and the stairs. Hence at that time women believed that linoleum and paint on the stairs was the most sanitary and clean method, even if they *could* afford carpet.

It had been my dream for many years, however, to cover my stairs with good, plain, red carpet, and just before the war commenced, my dream came true. My stairs, with their lovely red carpet, were my pride and joy, but now, to my horror, these children were running up and down them with cups of hot tea, dropping the sticky liquid all over my carpet. As a result, when I vacuumed the stairs, the vacuum took lumps of wool out of the carpet, leaving bald patches, and once again I had to swallow my wrath, which was like painful lumps in my throat.

What with the money I had spent in feeding and helping all the evacuees who came (and were still coming) to me, the war was a costly business. Each week I was spending more money than I could earn in the shop. Although my husband was working in the colliery, he did not contribute his wages to the upkeep of our home because, as he said, 'We've got to save this money for the future—the more money you have, the more you'll give away.' He was of the opinion that those of our visitors who were not "family" should be paying for their place in our home, and it annoyed him to see that I was being imposed upon.

I knew I would have to do something about my sister's neighbours. It was one thing to give free hospitality to my own family, but to be imposed upon by strangers (and strangers who, I knew, had the means to provide for their own comforts) was quite another thing. So after they had been with me for a month, and were showing no signs of wanting to leave, I once again took the law into my own hands, and went out and found a flat for them, in a fairly large house on the outskirts of Maesteg. I knew it would be rather costly, as it was well furnished, but I booked the place for them and went home to tell them the good news that they could move in immediately. They didn't seem overjoyed, but I told them that the people were expecting them that day, so they packed their things and left, without so much as a "thank you for all you've done." However I considered it thanks enough to be rid of them!

By now it was nearing Christmas again. My sister-in-law Evelyn, her mother and the children had gone back to Mitcham again to settle up some business concerning their butcher's shop; they had been told that everything was quiet in Mitcham and there had been no bombing even during the Battle of Britain. It was because Evelyn was away that I had had room for Violet and her family and neighbours, but now Evelyn and *her* family wanted to return to me for Christmas, and as I had promised my brother Garfield that I would take care of them throughout the war, I knew I would have to go out looking for accommodation for my sister's family.

Two doors lower down the street lived a nice family, a Mr. and Mrs. Lewis and their two unmarried sons. I went down to see them, and asked if they would rent me a bedroom and a living room for my sister, her husband and their two children. They said they had never let rooms to anyone, but I pointed out that this was wartime and we all had to do our bit to help the less fortunate; if they did this, they would be helping their country as well as helping me and my family. Then I added that I would see that they were compensated for any inconvenience; and as the house was rented, I would pay the full rent of the whole house to them each week. They agreed then to let my sister have their furnished living room on the ground floor, with the empty parlour as a bedroom, since they themselves lived in the basement.

To furnish the parlour for Violet, Ivor bought a complete

147

double bed, and I gave them the loan of a single bed for the children and all the bedding for both beds, which made them very comfortable there. I told them that we would supply them with their weekly goods from my shop until Fred could get work, and Fred could take all the coal he wanted from the coal-house at the bottom of my garden so that they could have a nice fire in their home to keep them warm and comfortable. They seemed very happy about these arrangements.

Then I went with my brother-in-law to the Council offices in Maesteg, and introduced him to Mr. Whomsley, the officer in charge of sustenance. I told Mr. Whomsley that a bomb had dropped in their street in Isleworth and they'd come to me for shelter, but they had no means of sustenance; could he help them? At that he said, to my brother-in-law, 'There is no record here of any bombs being dropped in that area. Why have you left your home?'

'To bring my wife and two children down here for safety,' Fred told him.

So Evelyn and her mother and the children were able to come back. Pearl for one, was delighted, because now she had got her little John back—my brother's baby son. He had been only a few weeks old when he first came to us at the beginning of the war, and he seemed more like our own child; he was two and a half years old now, and we had missed him very much when his mother took him back to Mitcham.

TWENTY TWO

That winter the snow was deep on the ground, and Mr. Thomas, who brought us our weekly supplies of butter and eggs from his base at Cardigan Stores, Clydach, had failed to get his van over the Cymmer mountain road, and had had to turn back. (The snow on the Cymmer road was frozen hard, and driving on it was much too dangerous.) All traffic had been stopped by the police, so there could be no distribution of the rationed goods until the roads were safe again.

One of the customers, from higher up Tonna Road, had twelve ration books with me; normally the family would have been prepared to manage as best they could until the supplies came in, but now they seemed to be under pressure and kept sending the children down every hour to ask, 'Has Mr. Thomas been? Mammy's waiting for her butter.' Eventually I decided to go up to their house to explain to their mother that the police had stopped all traffic on the Cymmer road, and as I went, I saw that an elderly woman who lived on the opposite side of the street had ploughed her way across to talk to my customer on her doorstep. This was most unusual, and I wondered why she had done so. The street was in a very bad state; it had not been cleaned, and the people who were sweeping their fronts had piled the snow so high in the gutter that the woman must have had great difficulty in getting through it. Her husband worked in an office; there were just two of them, and they were comfortably off as regards money, so they had built up a lovely home; for years now they had looked down their noses at the less elegant families across the road.

I already had my suspicions that something was not quite right; before the war my customer and her family ate only margarine, but now they were pestering me because the butter was a day late, and they were not at all bothered about the margarine. Still, it was not my business to ask why she wanted the butter so urgently. I said to her, 'Miriam, I'm sorry, but you'll have to wait like all the others until Mr. Thomas can get through. It's not my fault that it's

149

not in the shop. Everybody is waiting for eggs and butter and all the things they are entitled to.'

The next day was the same. The children were down every half hour of the day, and from my shop we could see that the elderly neighbour was crossing the road time after time to Miriam's home, so I knew she was responsible for the children being sent down to me. On Saturday Mr. Thomas managed to get through, and the supplies were all delivered; Miriam's children were the first in line to be served. Now Friday and Saturday were the two days allowed for customers to clear their bills, but these children were offering me not the ten pounds their mother owed me on her shop bill, but just the amount for the butter. I told them to go back and tell their mammy to pay her shop bill, then she could have all her rations together.

Soon they came back, saying, 'Mammy doesn't want anything this week, only her butter and marge.'

'Tell Mammy she can't have her butter and marge until she pays last week's bill,' I said. Next thing, their father came down, stuttering and stammering and banging the counter. He wanted his rations, he announced, and he was paying cash for them. I told him that they had already had all their rations, excepting the fats.

'Your wife carried enough food on "turn books" yesterday to feed you all next week,' I said. 'You are evidently not paying last week's bill, and it's clear I'm not likely to receive next week's money either. So until you pay for what you've already eaten, you'll not have your fat rations or anything more.'

'I'll go to the Food Office and report you,' he said.

'Do as you please,' I told him, 'but get out of my shop and let me get on with my work—supplying the people who *have* paid me!'

(I knew that even those people who normally paid me regularly could soon get into difficulties if I let their bills run over at any point—which didn't help either them or me.)

The man left my shop, caught the bus and went to Maesteg. He was back on the next bus, and proudly presented me with a letter of authority, ordering me to "hand over this man's rations at once", under threat of a visit from the officer in charge. I handed it back, and said, 'Go back on the next bus and give this letter back with my compliments! Tell him I take orders from no-one, and I shall welcome his visit!'

150

The irate customer looked surprised, and hesitated, uncertain as to what to do. He hadn't expected such a reply to the message he had brought me, but he took the letter, caught the bus and returned to the office in Maesteg. Later he came back again and called in at the shop to inform me, 'I took the letter back, and now you are for it!' meaning that I was in real trouble.

I carried on serving my customers, and some time later the inspector arrived at my shop. To my surprise he was one of those in whose company I had been the previous Saturday night, at a charity concert given by the Morriston Orpheus Choir from Swansea. But gone now was the friendly gentleman of the concert; here was a man full of authority and self-importance. My shop was empty of customers, and before discussing business, he took stock of all the goods on display.

'I see you've got a good stock in your shop,' he remarked.

'Yes, I have,' I said.

'It should include a good supply of butter and margarine and so on?'

'Yes,' I said. 'Mr. Thomas was unable to come over on Thursday to deliver the rationed goods, and many of the customers have not yet collected their fat rations.'

'Yes, but you should have quite a large quantity of butter etc over and above the customers' rations,' he suggested.

'No,' I replied. 'The government only allows me as much of the rationed goods as my customers' ration books cover. They don't even allow a little for loss of weight in cutting the food up into such small bits and pieces—and one has to be a magician today to handle these rations!'

'Oh, come, come, Mrs. Webb,' he said. 'What about all this man's rations? You've had all his butter for the past couple of years. What have you done with it?'

'Perhaps you'd better explain what you mean,' I demanded.

'Well,' he said, 'this man came down complaining that you won't give him his rations, and all he wants is his margarine. When I asked him "what about your butter", he said "we never eat butter". So if they don't eat butter, what have you done with all the butter they should have had since rationing started?'

'Firstly, I have not refused this man his rations,' I said. 'I merely told him that he must wait until he has paid for what they've had last week, and then they can have this week's supplies. But I'll let my book explain the rest of your questions.'

151

I opened my book at the man's account, and put it in front of the inspector. He was able to see, quite clearly, that the rations for all the twelve people in the man's family had been supplied, and paid for, each week—including their butter.

'Hmm. They're not bad payers, are they? They've paid every week so far,' he commented.

'Yes,' I agreed. 'But more importantly, as you will observe, their butter is on the bill, and they wouldn't have paid for it if they hadn't received it.'

'Then what are they doing with their butter?' he asked.

'I am only here to see that it is given out,' I told him. 'Not to ask questions about what they do with it when it is taken away. I assumed they had eaten their rations. And you can see that they've already carried away all the rest of this week's rationed goods, even though the stuff will not be paid for for another week. The only goods they are waiting for are the ones Mr. Thomas was unable to deliver on time, due to the bad weather, and those they will have when they pay the ten pounds for last week's goods. I have paid my travellers for these goods, and now the customers must pay me.—And until this man pays me the money, he will have nothing more in this shop.'

At this the inspector made to walk out of the shop, and he said, with a look of triumph on his face, 'You'll have your money now, Mrs. Webb. I'll put the fear of God into those people!' And with that, he was gone.

Some time passed before he returned, looking very pleased with himself. 'You'll have your money, Mrs. Webb,' he told me. 'They'll be down with the ten pounds. I've frightened the life out of them! And they've confirmed that a woman from across the road has been buying their butter off them, for a good price, throughout the war. Will you sign here, Mrs. Webb?' And he put a document on the counter in front of me, and pointed to the places where I should put my signature. I assumed that this was just to certify that the inspector had visited me, and that he was satisfied the people had not been deprived of their butter rations, and I was on the point of signing when a niggling doubt came into my mind, and made me stop. The print was too small for my sight, so I asked the inspector if he would kindly explain the reason why I had to sign this document. (It hadn't really occurred to me that this involved a Black Market offence; catching the two families would be a feather in the inspector's cap.)

'I've had a look at these people's home,' he said, 'and there's nothing there we can get from them, but I've been over to the other family's home, and there's plenty there we can have. It's a nice house, they own it, and we'll make the buggers pay!'

'You mean this will be a court case, and I will have to go to court?' I asked.

'Yes, Mrs. Webb, and we'll make the buggers squirm for what they've done.'

'Not with my help you won't,' I said. 'The people who sold the butter are very poor. They did wrong, I know, but it's not for me to punish them. And the people across the road, well, I agree they were greedy, and wrong in what they've done, but once again that's not my concern. They are elderly, and my neighbours, and I have to live in this street and earn a living for myself and my family. I will bring no disgrace or shame on my neighbours, you'll have to fight your own battles. I will not put my signature to these papers.'

The inspector said, 'I've got a good case here, but I can't do anything without your signature.'

'Then I'm afraid you'll have to do without it. Good day.'

He stormed, he banged the counter and was most abusive, but I turned a deaf ear to it all and walked into my sitting room. He shouted after me, 'I'll get you for this!' and I knew it was no idle threat; but I saw nothing of him after that until near the end of the war. (What occurred then, I will tell you later—he was not a man to forget his threat.)

*　　　*　　　*

My sister Violet, her husband Fred and their children had settled in very comfortably with Mr. and Mrs. Lewis, and Fred had obtained temporary employment as an extra postman over Christmas. After Christmas they moved to a furnished house in Bridgend, and both Violet and Fred went to work in the arsenal, Violet (who'd had a good education) as a supervisor, and Fred as a fireman. Nell, Fred's mother, had to stay in London because of her work, and to take care of the house, but as the Germans had been concentrating their bombing on the City of London, the suburb of Isleworth had been fairly peaceful.

Evelyn and her mother (who were also back with us, of course) told me that their part of Mitcham had also escaped bombing and had suffered no damage. Then Evelyn told me a very strange story about my brother Garfield. At that time everything to do with military matters was strictly hush hush—and much of it remained so for many years after the war. Certainly I might never have heard of this story if my brother had not been involved. This is how it was told to me:

Garfield, officially known as Sergeant Major Bowen, was in charge at Penlee Fort, Plymouth. He was a master gunner and responsible for the heavy guns firing across the Channel. Just after the fall of France he received secret information (not to be disclosed even to his men) that Britain was about to be invaded by the Germans; they hoped to surprise us by launching their invasion on the South Coast in the area where my brother's command lay. The experts worked out the only possible invasion dates from the tide and weather charts, and all the units along the coast, including my brother's men, were ordered to stand at the ready, near their guns, night and day (though the ordinary troops were still not told about the impending invasion.)

On the night when the invasion was expected, when they believed the Germans were coming in by barge and possibly then swimming ashore from the barges to avoid being seen by the sentries on shore, there was oil on the water. Somehow this was set on fire when there were men in the water, and the cries of the trapped men so upset the young officer in charge of the operation that he became almost insane. He had to be taken to hospital at once, but he was so violent that they could not get him into the ambulance. Now Garfield was very much loved by all his men, and regarded as a good and just Sergeant Major; he told the soldiers, 'Release my officer, and leave him to me,' then he put his hand on the young man's shoulder and said, 'Come with me, mate.'

Garfield and the officer climbed into the back of a jeep, and the driver started to take them to the hospital, but on the way another jeep crashed into the back of the vehicle, killing the young officer and severely injuring my brother. Garfield was in hospital for quite a long time, and I never knew the full extent of his injuries, but Evelyn said they were serious, and his whole body was encased in plaster of paris for many months. Neither Evelyn nor I knew that Garfield was in hospital until he was due to be released, because he had insisted that his letters to his wife and me were to be taken to Penlee Fort to have its stamp on them, and we were not told of his accident or his whereabouts until Evelyn was officially

154

Ivan aged 4.

The Author's Mother, Mrs. Rachel Bowen
with her second husband D.C. Thomas
"Dai" and their little dog, "Dai".

Alfred Webb with part of his family, from left to right – Mr. Webb, daughter Dolly,
Will, daughter-in-law Rachel, son Ivor and daughter Winnie. Picnicking in Mr. Webb's
field which is now Caerau Park.

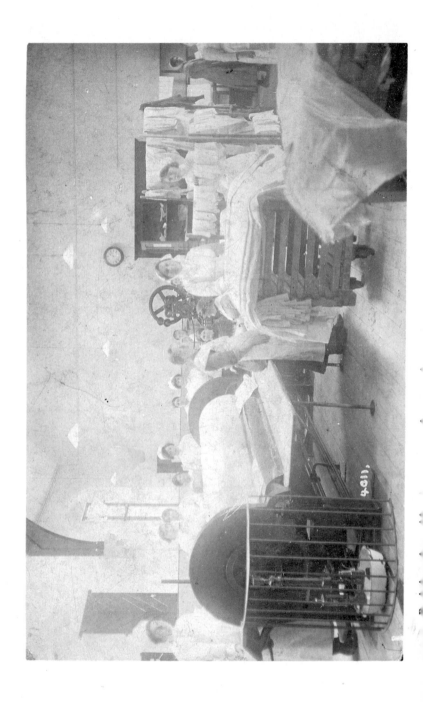

Pearl and Jack's introduction to the grey skies and the White Cliffs of Dover on our return to England, (S.S. Hobsons Bay).

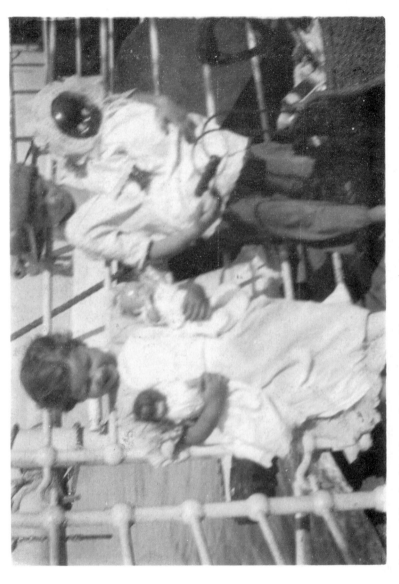

Jack and Pearl taking first prize in a competition on board the S.S. Hobsons Bay with their interpretation of "Married Bliss".

notified that he was being released from hospital and returned to his home in Mitcham. It was for this reason that Evelyn had stayed in London for a few weeks, while she nursed my brother back to health, but now he was back on duty and Evelyn was with me again.

Sadly, it seems that Garfield's injuries contributed to the onset of the cancer which developed some years later, and from which he died at the early age of fifty-two. He had served his country for thirty-six years.

One day a man called at the shop and put a parcel on the counter, saying, 'For Mrs. Webb, with compliments.' I hesitated to handle the parcel at first, because it had been given to me with no indication as to its place of origin or sender, but a customer, anxious to know what it contained, said, 'I'll open it for you. Let's see what's in it!' and she proceeded to open the large parcel. It held many, many yards of beautiful parachute silk, which we assumed had come from the German parachutes that had come down over Caerau. This was indeed a treasure, as clothing material was hard to come by during the war, and could only be got with the clothing coupons included in our ration books. We were only allowed a very few per month.

As there were so many yards of parachute silk, I divided it—some for myself and some for my neighbours—and so we were all able to make some nice underwear for ourselves and our children. One day Jack came home with another great treasure, this time from the river! It was an old car tyre that had washed down in the river and got tangled in some brambles on the side of the river bank. Jack said, 'Mammy, I thought this would be handy for Daddy to "tap" his working boots.' So this too was cut up into parts and divided amongst ourselves and our neighbours. This was how we helped one another during the war; nothing was wasted, we shared everything.

Mention of the parachute silk reminds me that it was time now for Jack to start his apprenticeship as a mechanical engineer with Shepherds in Bridgend. On the day when the three German parachutists were caught, I had been talking with Mr. Mellhuish, one of my travellers, who traded as "Diamond of Bridgend", and he had promised to have a word with Mr. Shepherd and make sure that there was a place reserved for Jack when he was old enough. Now that day had come.

Also, the experiment of the "lollipop lady" which had started in Caerau, had now spread over a much wider area, and the people, mostly women or old age pensioners (because the men had been called up) wore white coats, as I had worn my white shop coat when directing the children across the road.

TWENTY THREE

One day the doctor called in and asked me to arrange to go to the clinic in Maesteg. It meant hiring a car, as my body had now filled up with water—what we called "dropsy" in those days; I was suffering from toxaemia in pregnancy. I had already been in bed for a few weeks because of this toxaemia and none of my clothes would fit my body, so my mother borrowed two extra large outsized lightweight dressing gowns from the neighbours. One was put on back to front and fastened at the back, while the other was put on in the normal way and pinned in front, so that they covered me when I went in the car to go to the clinic.

When the nurse came to collect me from the waiting room and take me in to see the doctors, Nurse Aubrey was in the clinic, and insisted on going in with me. The doctor told her, 'There's no need for you to come in,' but she said, 'I'm her nurse, and Mrs. Webb is going to engage me for the confinement.'

'No, Nurse Aubrey,' he said, 'she won't be engaging you.'

I could see that Nurse Aubrey was hurt, and I told the doctor, 'She was with me when my first two children were born. She's a very good nurse, and I trust her. I'd like to have her again.'

However the doctor explained to Nurse Aubrey, 'Mrs. Webb will not require a nurse. We will probably have to take her in to hospital shortly, to await the birth of the child.'

I asked the doctor if he would give me some clothing coupons, so that I could buy clothes for the baby, as I understood that extra coupons were only given to expectant mothers at the clinic.

'Mrs. Webb, I don't want you to make any preparations for this baby,' he said. But I pleaded with him to give me some coupons. 'If I don't prepare for the baby,' I told him, 'it would seem as if I didn't want the child, and I do, I very much want this baby.' So he gave me the necessary coupons, but told me that I should explain to the shopkeeper, when I purchased the baby clothes, that the doctor had said I might not need them, and ask if she would take them back if they did prove to be unnecessary.

157

I insisted on them taking me straight to "Babyland" with the coupons, and there I told Mrs. Williams in the shop that I wanted a complete layette of baby clothes, for night and day. She told her assistants to bring the clothes to the counter so that I could choose what I wanted, but when I saw that they were all stamped with the "Utility" mark, I told Mrs. Williams, 'You can take them all back. I want pre-war garments. I'm not buying these with Provident cheques, I'm paying cash.' (Utility clothes were skimpy and of poor quality, and shopkeepers had to sell them to the people who were paying by Provident cheque, because otherwise they would lose too much money on the sale. The shopkeeper had to pay the Provident company a percentage on every garment sold, and so would lose approximately two pounds in every ten poundsworth of goods they supplied.) Mrs. Williams signalled to the girl to go to another room, to fetch some other baby clothes, and I had all I required of pre-war, beautiful baby garments; I didn't follow the doctor's instructions and ask her to take them back if they were not required, as I knew I would do everything I could to keep this child.

A few nights later, something happened during the night that alarmed both my husband and I. Our bed was swamped with water. The nearest midwife to my home was Nurse Bevington-Rees, who came quickly when my husband told her what had happened. She told me not to worry, everything was in order and she had phoned for the doctor. It was Dr. Sinclair who came, accompanied by a new young doctor, Dr. Murphy, who was just over from Ireland. The two doctors stayed in my house for the next few days, along with Nurse Bevington-Rees, and at night Dr. Sinclair slept, fully clothed, on the side of my bed, while Dr. Murphy sat on a chair at the other side. Thus we spent every night from Friday till Tuesday, and in the morning, after a breakfast prepared for him by Nurse Bevington-Rees, Dr. Murphy would go to Jack's bed to sleep, after Jack had left it for the day. Ivor, who did not go to work during that period, slept with Ivan, and Nurse Bevington-Rees waited on the doctors, preparing their meals and their baths and attending to any other needs.

On the Tuesday morning, six weeks before the date on which my baby was due to be born, Dr. Sinclair told me that they were going to deliver the baby that day.

'We mustn't wait any longer,' he said. 'We're going to give you "Twilight sleep". This is what the queen had when her babies

158

were born, and it costs fifty pounds, so you're a very special and honoured little lady today.' (The queen he was speaking of is now the Queen Mother, of course.)

I kept my eyes closed while the baby was being delivered. I could hear everything the doctors and the nurse were saying, but I could feel nothing. There was no chloroform, and I couldn't tell what "twilight sleep" was, but I heard Dr. Sinclair say that it was "a double breech birth" and add, 'Thank God we didn't wait any longer.' Then he said to me, 'You've got a lovely little baby girl. Call her Elizabeth, after my mother!'

'No, doctor,' I said, 'she's already been named—Elaine Margaret.'

'I've never heard that name before—Elaine. Where did you get that from?'

'When I was a little girl, there were two beautiful film stars. One was called "Pearl" and one "Elaine"; I've already got Pearl, and now I've got Elaine. The name means "precious gift of God", and this is indeed a precious gift from God.'

After the baby was washed and dressed and given to me, rolled up in an eiderdown, I was told not to let anyone handle her; no-one was even to pick her up. I noticed a thick collar of cotton wool and bandage round her neck, but I didn't ask questions because I didn't realise that there was anything wrong. I thought the collar was to support her neck, as she was only six pounds in weight and six weeks premature. When they allowed my husband to come into the bedroom to see the baby, he exclaimed, 'Oh! She's too pretty to live!' Her eyes were wide open and were very blue, and her head was covered in fair curls; with her little pink cheeks she looked like a wax doll, not a newly-born baby.

Now the doctors were preparing to leave the room, prior to leaving the house, and Nurse Bevington-Rees said, 'Well, Dr. Sinclair, you never thought you'd be having your breakfast in Tonna Road for the last five days!' Dr. Sinclair stopped, looked back at me, and smiled, then said, 'No, nurse. And I never thought I'd be sleeping with a woman in Tonna Road, either!' And, roaring with laughter, the two doctors left the room. As they went out, they told the children downstairs that they had a beautiful baby sister, and they told Pearl, 'She's exactly like you!'

I was very happy, for now I had two lovely dark boys and two lovely fair girls. When they saw their little sister, the children were overjoyed, and Pearl said, 'Everybody in the world must envy us

159

today.' She was even sorry for our awkward shopkeeper neighbours, because they had never known the joy of having a baby in their home.

But our joy was to be short-lived. No visitors were allowed up in the bedroom, in case they tried to pick the baby up, and although it was May and the weather was warm, she had to be left absolutely quiet, lying on the bed, wrapped in the eiderdown (a single-bed eiderdown, not a cot-sized one). The doctor had been calling day and night the whole time, but no-one told me I was going to lose my little girl. She didn't cry, but just made a little faint moan, and on the eighth day, as I was sitting up, nursing her, still wrapped in her eiderdown, I was aware that things were not what they should be.

Her eyes were unblinking, wide open and staring into my face, and that gentle little moan seemed to be getting fainter. I remembered the time when I had sat by my father's dead body, staring into his face and saying, 'I'm never going to forget you,' and I thought to myself, 'Is my little girl staring at me because she's trying to tell me she'll never forget me?' I pleaded and pleaded with God not to take my little girl. 'Let me keep her,' I prayed. 'I have waited a long time for her, and I can't bear to let her go!'

I could see no improvement in the baby; there seemed to be no change in her one way or the other, but I knew she was slipping away, and I turned now to the mother of Jesus and prayed that she would intercede for me and beg her son to let me keep my little one. The doctor had come by in the morning but though he had looked at the baby, he said nothing to me. However he had told my husband downstairs (so I was later informed) that once the baby's little moan stopped, she would die. Meanwhile I watched my little one, pleading with Jesus and Mary to save her. At last her little breathing stopped, and I knew she was gone.

I didn't tell anyone, I just kept her in my arms. If anyone came up into the bedroom, I said, 'She's sleeping,' and sent them back downstairs. When the doctor came in the evening, I was still sitting up in bed, with her in my arms. He knew she was dead, and he said, 'How long?'

'Six hours,' I said.

'Why haven't you told anyone?' he asked.

'Because they'll only take her away, and I don't want them to take her,' I told him.

He went downstairs and told the family that the baby had died. Pearl ran upstairs, screaming, but didn't come into my room. She went into her own room, turned the key, and stayed there all night, crying; no-one could coax her to come out or go in to comfort her.

My mother came up to the bedroom and tried to persuade me to give the baby to her. She asked me, 'Why didn't you tell anyone the baby had died? I would have come up straightaway.'

'I didn't want anyone to know. I wanted to keep her myself,' I said.

'Don't upset yourself, Rit,' my mother said. 'Think of me. I lost six little ones, so I know how you feel.'

'But this one is mine, Mam,' I said, 'and I can't let them take her away.'

The undertaker brought a little white coffin, and I insisted they put her christening robe on her; it was silk and lace. When the man placed her in the coffin and put that on a little trestle, I told him he was to leave it by the side of my bed, which he did. Pearl still couldn't be persuaded to come out of her bedroom; I could hear her from my room, but I couldn't go to her, as I couldn't put my feet on the floor. I called to her, but she couldn't hear me, she was sobbing so hard.

The following day, at dinnertime, Pearl had still not come out of her bedroom, and had had nothing to eat or drink. My mother tried to persuade her, but knew it was no use appealing to her by saying, 'You'll die if you don't stop crying,' so she used other tactics.

'Pearl, your mother has had nothing to eat or drink since yesterday morning,' she said. 'If she doesn't have food soon, she'll die. You don't want to lose your mother as well, do you?'

At that Pearl said, 'If Mammy will promise to eat food, I'll come out and eat some food with her.' So then a tray was brought up to my bedroom and Pearl came in, and we ate together.

Dr. Murphy came in and saw my little girl in the coffin, and cried as though his heart would break. He had been calling my little baby 'Princess' for the eight days he had been coming in to see us, and he would come in and say, 'How's my little princess today?' Now here was his 'little princess' in her coffin. He couldn't have taken it harder if it was his his own child. He told me, 'I will never understand God taking this little one.'

I told him how I had prayed for God to spare this child to me, and he said, 'I've just come from a house now where the mother has been delivered of twins. They already had about ten children, and could easily have done without the twins, but God has left them and taken this little one who could have had everything.' He shook his head and repeated, 'I'll never understand.'

Because it was wartime, there were no men left to dig graves in the cemetery. My husband tried to buy a family burial plot, but was told that he could not do so because of the war, and then he was told that he could not have a grave for a child either, but would have to wait until there was a funeral for an adult, because then an existing grave would have to be opened. After that funeral they would be able to bury our little one before reclosing the grave. Then my husband asked the sexton if it was possible for him to have a grave which he could show me when I was well enough to go down to the cemetery; he said he would pay for this, however much it might cost, because our baby had not been stillborn, she had been eight days old and we didn't want her to be buried in an unknown grave.

'I want a Christian burial for her,' Ivor said. 'I don't want her little coffin smuggled into someone else's grave at night. And I want a funeral and a funeral service. We want to know where she is buried, and we can't do that if she's in someone else's grave.'

The sexton took Ivor to a little grassy patch and told him. 'This is a closed grave. It hasn't belonged to anyone for many, many years, and we have buried five babies there recently. If you like, we can put your little child in there. You pay us a sum of money, and we open the grave and put your baby there; then you can call that grave your own. But on no account must you ever put a stone or an ornament on it—nothing other than flowers.'

Ivor had to agree to that. I was unable to go to the baby's funeral because I was heavily sedated and not allowed out of bed.

The baby's death was a tragic loss, and it took many hours for us, as a family, to accept it. Pearl, in particular, was deeply affected by her "child's first grief."

162

TWENTY FOUR

One day, when I was back again in my shop, Mr. Warren, who was a commercial traveller for a large wholesaler in Cardiff, called in at the shop on his regular monthly visit. As was our custom, I paid him in cash for the last order of goods I had received from his firm; this was quite a large sum of money. Then I put the receipted bill on the file, and he wrote down my new order for the next month's supplies.

Mr. Warren lived in Bridgend, and he told me that a story had gone around the town concerning a woman in Caerau who had spotted three German parachutists coming down from a plane over one of the Caerau mountains. Because it was wartime, and details like names were not allowed to be disclosed, the woman's name had not been released—'But we all wondered who it could be,' he said, so I told him it was me. After that I had to tell him the whole story from beginning to end.

When I had finished, we shook hands and he went on to the next shop, but some time later, when I was busy tidying up the counter just before closing the shop, I found that Mr. Warren had not taken the money order with him. I had no idea of his address in Bridgend, so I couldn't contact him, and I was very worried, because it was a large amount. I put it away safely, hoping that he would come back to collect it once he had realised his loss, but time went by and still he hadn't returned. I left the money where I had put it, and soon forgot all about it. In fact, by the following month, when Mr. Warren came on his next visit, the lost money had gone completely out of my mind, and not even seeing him helped to jog my memory. Mr. Warren did not mention any loss; and it was not until later, when Ivor and I were discussing the day's business, that Ivor asked, 'Did you give Mr. Warren the money he left on the counter?'

'Oh no,' I gasped. 'I forgot all about it, Ivor!'

After that I decided to attach a note to Mr. Warren's next bill, so that when the goods came in and I had to pay for them, I would be reminded to tell him about his lost money. Another month passed, and Mr. Warren called as usual. He came up to the counter and stood there, and I said, 'Before we discuss anything else, there's something we must settle.'

'There wasn't anything wrong with the order, was there, Mrs. Webb?' he asked, looking worried. I could see he was afraid I had a complaint.

'No, Mr. Warren,' I reassured him. 'I'm the one who has a confession to make. I should have told you about his last month, but I forgot completely until after you'd gone. Two months ago you receipted this bill I have in my hand—but you forgot to pick up your money!'

Mr. Warren staggered like a drunken man; then he sat down on a chair and called for water. I handed him a glass.

'Was it here I left it?' he said. 'Thank God for that. When I got home that day and counted my money, I could see that there was a large sum missing. I'd visited several shops that paid me the same amount of money, and they had all got receipted bills, so I didn't know *where* I had left it. I told my wife, "I hope to God I've left it at Mrs. Webb's, I know then that it will be safe," but when you didn't say anything about it on my next visit, I thought I couldn't have left it here.'

'Why didn't you ask me then, Mr. Warren?' I enquired.

'I couldn't,' he said. 'If I hadn't left it here, then I might have offended you, and I couldn't risk that.'

'You wouldn't have offended me,' I told him. 'In fact, you would have saved me a lot of anxiety, because the thought that I had caused you worry by not mentioning the money was worrying me! I would have phoned you, but I had no idea where you live, and I wouldn't risk phoning your firm.'

'Thank God you didn't phone them,' he said, 'or I would have had the sack, and I'd rather have lost the money than my job!'

It would have been a tremendous amount of money for him to have lost, and he told me he was going home a very happy man; not only that, his wife would be delighted when he told her that all was well.

When he called the following month, Mr. Warren looked very sad, and I noticed that he was in deep mourning. He told me that his nine-year-old son had had an accident; the accident was very slight, but it had resulted in the boy's death. Mr. Warren was heartbroken, and the loss affected him terribly, but I thanked God that I had at least been able to see that his money was returned safely so that he did not have that anxiety to add to the devastation and sorrow of losing his little boy so suddenly.

*　　*　　*

There were posters everywhere warning us that "careless talk could lose the war", but though we seldom discussed anything concerning the war when customers came into the shop, there were times when Lord Haw Haw's broadcasts had come near to undermining people's morale, and frightened women needed a little reassurance. They would bring up the subject of Lord Haw Haw's recent propaganda while they stood in the shop, waiting, and once I heard one woman remark, 'He said the Germans would soon be marching through our valleys, but the Germans won't have *my* children if they come here.'

'No! And they won't have *our* children either,' said the other mothers, in chorus. 'We'll poison them first, rather than let those Germans get hold of them.' They went on to discuss how they would protect their families and themselves if the propaganda proved to be true.

'I have some pills in the house,' said one woman, 'and before the Germans got anywhere near my children, I would give them each a pill, and then there would be one for my husband and one for myself. The children would go first, and then us.'

I didn't want to join in any discussion of this sort, yet I knew that they were waiting for someone to give them a word of encouragement, so I asked them if they had listened to Mr. Churchill's latest speeches on their wireless sets.

'Haven't you heard him declare "We will fight them on the hilltops, we will fight them in the valleys, we will fight them on the beaches"? You've seen our Home Guard in action, and you know we Welsh don't give up easily. So put your trust in our Home Guard for the safety of your children, don't talk about horrible things like poison and pills. And you mothers who have boys serving in the Army—they are putting their lives at risk to prevent the Germans coming to our shores. Don't let them down by being defeatists, just remember our valleys have bred some of the finest men and boys in the world. They won't let you down, so don't you let them down.'

165

It seemed that the Germans were now trying invasion tactics by air, because they were dropping thousands of flares over the mountains, hoping the lights would guide them, so that they could come down silently and take us by surprise. During the First World War our mountains had been the greatest defence for the valleys of Wales, but just after 1918, in a wonderful feat of engineering, roads had been cut, up, over and around them, opening up all the heads of the valleys and giving access from one valley to the next.

All the valley roads met at the topmost point of one of the highest mountains in the area, and there, at this crossroads, the soldiers had built a lookout post, from which they could command a view of the whole of the Rhondda valley, as well as of the tops of the mountains. When the German planes came over, dropping their flares and hoping that the fire from these would set alight the grass and heather, giving them light by which to drop their invasion troops, the courageous local men of the Home Guard came to our defence, and put the flares out as fast as they fell. Once again the Germans had failed to penetrate the defences of our island.

However, although the local people believed themselves to be safe in these valleys, and children and other evacuees were sent here, the Afan and Llynfi districts were said to be very high on the list of danger areas if it came to a German invasion, and because of this our local Home Guard was a particularly well-trained force, always on the alert. It was the Home Guard which kept the valleys safe, because the Forces did not have enough troops to spare for that duty. The military work the men did was voluntary, and was in addition to the nine hours they spent each day deep down in the bowels of the earth, digging coal. It was this very hard mining work that gave them the strong sinews and muscles in their arms and legs that they needed to enable them to scramble over the mountains on foot. The new roads had to curve along the hillsides, and stretched for four miles or more from the valley up to the top of the mountains, so climbing up the steep mountainsides, using all their skill and muscle power, was a much quicker way to travel.

Meanwhile the nearby town of Swansea was being very heavily bombed by the German planes, and from the oil that was on our windows one morning, we knew that the bombers had blown up the oil refinery there. It was terrible to hear the planes droning

166

over our valley, knowing that they were bringing destruction to our families and friends in Swansea; even when we were not afraid for our own lives, we lived in fear for the others who were dear to us.

My next adventure began early one cold, dark morning. My husband caught the train to Bridgend; he had now been put off from the colliery due to the increasingly serious condition of his lungs, which were full of stone dust. He was still determined to do his bit for the war effort, and had a new job working in the arsenal. Jack had got up to go to his new apprenticeship as a fitter and turner with Shepherd's in Bridgend. We lived in such fear of enemy destruction in those years that you carried the fear in your heart whenever you had to say goodbye to your children, whether they were going to school or to work. Something might happen during the course of the day, they might be killed or injured, and you might never see them again. So I remained on the pavement until the bus taking Jack to work had gone out of sight, then I returned to my basement flat.

I had left the side entrance door open, and I left it unlocked when I went back in, because it would soon be time to call my other two children down, ready to get them off to their school in Bridgend. However I had only just gone through the living room door and closed it behind me when I heard a loud knock on the kitchen door. I was rather surprised by this, but I thought it might be a customer who wanted to be served with something from the shop before going to work, so I answered the knock.

It was still dark outside, and in the light from the house I could see a tall, thin man standing there. He was holding an empty tin in his hand, and he held it out to me, saying something—though I could not quite make out what. His thick, long coat reached right down to his ankles, and I could see that his feet were bare inside his down-at-heel shoes, while his soft hat was drawn down to his eyes. He was looking downwards, towards the ground, and the thick muffler wound around his neck and mouth prevented me from seeing any of his face. He repeated the same word, which sounded to me like "water".

I knew this was no customer or neighbour, but a "strange man", of the type described in the secret Government warnings sent to shopkeepers, and here I was, all by myself. My backyard and bakehouse were surrounded by an eight-foot-high wall; the stout oak door leading to the lane was shut, and the lane and fields

167

around my premises were dark. I had to pull my wits together quickly, and call to mind what the leaflets had advised: "Don't show fear, act normally," and in order to cover my confusion I started to talk to the man, very rapidly. He was looking into my warm, lighted, living room, and as it was a very cold morning, I said to him, 'Do you want hot water to make tea?'

He did not reply, so I asked, 'Would you like to come inside and have some breakfast, then?' At that he walked inside without answering, took a chair and sat right beside the fire. I realised that he must have been inside my yard all the while when I was seeing my husband and son off to work, but he had concealed himself until I came back in and closed the door. He didn't remove his hat and scarf, but held his big coat tightly around him with one arm while he warmed the other hand by the fire. Quickly I poured out a hot cup of tea with sugar and milk and put it on the table beside him, then, since he was looking at the remains of my husband's and son's breakfast, which were still on the table, I asked him if he would like something to eat, as he must be very hungry.

He just nodded, and made a growling sound that I gathered was supposed to mean "yes". I went into the kitchenette, cooked him some bacon and eggs, and covered a few slices of bread with margarine to go with it. Inwardly I was very frightened, but I tried as hard as I could to keep control of myself and act as normally as possible. It was now that my years of living in the Australian bush, feeling constant fear and anxiety and learning to live with it, helped me. I kept a calm composure on the outside, while inside I kept my fear suppressed just as I had while living in our tin shack, amidst poisonous snakes, strange threatening creatures, and primitive aborigines.

As I prepared breakfast for the stranger, I silently prayed for God's help in this situation. I didn't turn my back on the man for one second, but made sure that I could observe him at all times—even from my place at the cooker in the kitchenette I could keep a constant eye on him.

Evelyn and her mother had gone back to Mitcham for a few days, because it was necessary for Mrs. Hall to keep in touch with her butchery business. This had been left to her by her husband, and she had appointed her married sons as managers of the various butchers' shops, but she still kept a regular check on the business and went home every so often to collect her share of the profits and see the money was banked. Unfortunately, because she and Evelyn were absent, I was now alone in the basement with this weird, forbidding stranger, and my two youngest children were asleep in their beds at the top of the house, with only a few closed doors to protect them. My one greatest fear was that they would wake and come downstairs.

The man kept his eyes on me all the time, and we watched each other so hard that the tension became almost unbearably claustrophobic, but I knew I had to stay with him. I was afraid that if I attempted to go upstairs to warn the children it would make him suspicious, and I couldn't risk that. I did have one feeble hope to hang on to, though; if I could keep him there until half past eight, when the Tyderwen school children would be coming up the back lane on their way to school, then Mr. Will Griffiths, the school caretaker, who usually went ahead of the children to light the boilers, might see my side door unlocked and call in for a cup of coffee. (Will Griffiths was a friend of Ivor's, who lived on the other side of the valley, and he was in the habit of calling in for a morning cup of coffee on the way to the school.) I prayed most earnestly that God would send Will Griffiths that morning.

After the man had finished his food, he began to get very uneasy. He could see that it was getting light, and I think he wanted to disappear, but I kept supplying him with fresh cups of tea, while I talked to him.

'You're working on the school, are you?' I said, and then went on, without giving him a chance to answer, 'Painting the railings, is it?' (I knew full well that the school railings would never be painted in wartime, and furthermore Will Griffiths was the school handyman and would have told me if there was any work being done at the school, but it was something to say, so that the man would think I did not suspect that anything was wrong.)

When the man showed signs of getting up, I said, 'It's all right; keep warm here by the fire. You can't get into the school yet, the gates are not open until nine o'clock. I'll let you know when they open, don't worry,' I promised him, 'and then you won't have to hang about on the pavement in the cold. It's a very bitter, frosty morning. If you're working on the school, then you'll need lunch, won't you? I'll cut you some bread and cheese.' I had to use our rationed food to do this, but it was worth the sacrifice if I could keep him until Mr. Griffiths came.

Deep inside, I was shaking with fear that Will Griffiths would pass by this morning without calling, as he often did when he knew Ivor was at work, and I was trying to will him to call in. I kept saying to God, 'Please don't let Mr. Griffiths pass my door—send him in.' Then, after what seemed like hours of anxiety and fear, I finally heard footsteps in the back yard, and I silently said, 'Oh, thank you, God! You've answered my prayer!'

The man got suddenly agitated and jumped up from his chair. I put my hand on his arm and assured him, 'Don't be frightened, it's just our friend. He's come with the key to open the school, so now you'll be able to go in and start your work.'

Mr. Griffiths usually walked in without ceremony, but this time I wanted to alert him beforehand to the fact that something was wrong, so I called out to him loudly as he came through the yard, 'Come in, Mr. Griffiths, and meet our visitor. He's come to paint the school railings.'

Will opened the door and walked into the room, but instead of sitting down for a cup of coffee as usual, he looked hard at the man.

'Have you got the school key with you, Will?' I asked, knowing that he had, but knowing too that asking him about it would alert him to the fact that this was no expected visitor. 'Will you go up now and open the gates?' I went on. 'This young man has been waiting for a long time for the school to open up. You go now, while I cut him some bread and cheese to put in his pocket.'

Will looked at me, and said, 'You all right?'

'Yes. Hurry, Will, I'll see you later.'

He knew what I meant, and hurried up to the school where he got on the phone at once and called the police. Meanwhile I began to cut some bread and cheese for the man, working very slowly, and making the excuse that I had to look for some paper to wrap it in, in order to give Will and the police a chance to come down. By now the man was extremely restless, and I knew I wasn't going to keep him there much longer. I packed up the bread and cheese, and he snatched it up off the table without a word, and left the house.

I knew that once Will had alerted the police over the phone, it would only be three minutes before they arrived in their car, and they wouldn't give the man time to get away.

Later that same day, during the dinner hour, Will came down to tell me what had happened. 'The police picked the man up just a few yards outside your side entrance,' he said. 'Underneath that

Pearl's first day in Bryncethir (left of middle row). Mr. Jones is the headmaster.

Neighbours from the bottom end of Tonna Road. V.E. Celebrations, 1945.

greatcoat he was stark naked! He had escaped from the prisoner of war camp at Island Farm in Bridgend.' Will went on to tell me that it was believed that the young German had been walking all through the night, and had followed the railway line and the river up to Caerau, hoping to lose himself in the mountains; but then hunger and extreme cold had drawn him to my house.

I thanked God, despite the ordeal I had endured, that he had come to me and that I had given him a warm meal and some comfort, for whoever he was, he was some mother's son, and it was better that he should go back to the prisoner of war camp than freeze to death on the mountains. It seemed that he had believed that he could escape if he got over the mountains, not realising that in our valleys one mountain just leads over into another valley, and so on and so on.

As for me, as soon as the escaped prisoner had gone out through my door, I had locked and barred it, and collapsed on the settee. I was finally overcome by the fear I had been suppressing all that morning.

TWENTY FIVE

I had not yet got over losing my little baby girl, and I often suffered from a deep depression as a result of her death; I knew I would have to get myself out of this, and so one night I prayed ardently to God to lift me out of this terrible feeling of loss.

'If I could only see my little girl and know that she's happy,' I said to the Lord. 'Because at night I am haunted by the thought that my baby is alone and crying.'

That night, following the heart-cry of that prayer, a strange thing happened. I swear it wasn't a dream. I was spiritually transported to a place that was warm—not hot like the blazing, uncomfortable heat of Australia. The road I travelled on was unmade and sandy, the earth was of a reddish colour, in keeping with the warmth that I felt around me, and I was not alone on it—though I couldn't see my escort.

We walked to a farm gate, where we stopped. The gate was wooden, rough and handmade, just as you would find on a farmer's land. I rested my elbows on the top of the gate and looked up at the beautiful field that lay beyond, its short green grass full of little daisies. The field was long and narrow, and each side of it was edged with cherry trees, full of blossoms that seemed to spread out, throwing a shade over the expanse of grass. It was a lovely sight.

Then I felt the presence of my unseen escort over my left shoulder, and higher up the field I saw two forms emerge from what must have been a gap in the cherry trees. They were dressed in summer dresses of pure white. The taller one was a young girl of about twenty-two, with long fair hair, and as they came closer, I recognised her as Irene Hoskins, my school friend, who had died as the result of an accident back in 1926 (when she *was* twenty-two). By her side, holding her left hand as they came towards me, was my little girl, with her little silvery curls tossing and her eyes as blue as a bluebag—as were the older girl's. The pair could have been taken for mother and daughter, but I knew it was my little Elaine.

As they neared the gate they were both laughing and seemed very happy, and the voice over my shoulder said, quite clearly, 'Do you still want to take her back to that cold world?' I knew it was our Lord speaking to me, although I could not see Him, and I shouted in reply, 'No! No! No!' Three times I cried out, each time ephasizing the "no".

Then the scene changed, and I was alone, though still on that sandy road. I looked around me, not knowing where to go from there, when I saw my mother's sister, Margaret Harris coming towards me. She was just as I had known her when I was a young child and she was a lady doctor in Blackwood, and she called out to me, 'Ritty, what are you doing here?'

'Oh Bopa, I am here on a visit,' I cried, using the old Welsh name. She raised her hand and pointed to a row of little houses, of the sort that would today be called "old people's bungalows" (though there were no such houses in existence during the 1940s.) Aunt Margaret pointed out several houses and told me the names of those of my long-dead cousins who lived there.

'And this is mine,' she told me, pointing to the one that was her own. Next she pointed lower down the row, at another little bungalow. 'We are keeping that one for your mother, when she comes to us,' she said.

Then I found myself back in my bedroom. It had all been too vividly real to have been simply a dream, and from that moment on, my depression and my sorrow left me. I was content to leave my precious little girl in her heavenly home.

*   *   *

I mentioned earlier that I had volunteered to take part in the scheme for hospitality to the troops organised by Lady Frances Rider and Miss Fry; this had now progressed to the point where I received a telegram stating that they were sending me a young soldier from Newcastle who wanted to spend his fortnight's leave in Wales. I had to rearrange the bedrooms to accommodate this young man because I knew my "evacuees" would be back from Mitcham in a day or so, and I had to keep sufficient room for them to sleep.

The young soldier was tired after his journey on the night he arrived, and he asked me if I would mind if he went to bed early. I showed him up the two flights of stairs to the bedrooms, and told him that he could either take the small room with just a single bed, or he could share the bigger bedroom with my eldest son. Our visitor had already taken a liking to Jack, who was only a few years younger than himself, so he chose to sleep in Jack's room.

'I am used to company,' he explained, 'so I would prefer to share with your son.'

I left him, and went back down to the basement, where my newly-returned evacuees were all sitting round the fire with the rest of us, telling us tales of London. They said it was still very quiet around Mitcham; there had been no bombing near their homes, and if it stayed like that, they said there would be no reason why they couldn't go back home to live for the rest of the war. However they said they would wait for a while before going back.

The war was well on into its third year now. The Battle of Britain, fought in the skies over Southern England, had proved to the Germans that our British Air Force was superior to theirs, and now it was Germany which was suffering the battering that we had previously had to endure. The British were teaching the Germans that they had been wrong in believing what Hitler had told them—that they would win the war because "Might was Right", They thought they were sure to win because they had a mighty army, but we taught them that they were wrong; "Right was Might", and God was on our side.

On this particular night Jack was down in the basement with us, busy with one of his "experiments". Our wireless set was our only means of obtaining news, and our information regarding the war was relayed to us via what we called "a plug in the wall." We paid a modest two shillings a week to the relay company for this service, and the plug was fixed to the window sill, inside the living room. It couldn't be moved to any other room, so Jack was experimenting to see if he could listen to the programmes on the wireless through his headphones when he was in bed. He had the headphones fixed over his bed, with a wire coming through his bedroom window, down the outside wall and into the living room. So far he hadn't been able to hear the wireless programmes in this way, but he was still tinkering with the equipment, hoping to make it work by the time he went to bed, so that he could listen.

Ivor and I were discussing the hospitality scheme with our evacuees as they had not heard about it in Mitcham. 'I was a little anxious about the type of soldiers they would send me,' I said. 'But we are very pleased indeed with this young man. I must say he is well-spoken and well-groomed. He has evidently been well brought up, and we are very happy to have him staying with us. We only hope that he will enjoy his stay as much as we will enjoy having him.'

'I can teach him to box with my boxing gloves, can't I?' Ivan chirped in.

For the benefit of any young soldiers coming to stay with us, I had bought a good selection of games—for instance, a mahogany skittle board with a pole in the middle and a ball attached to a chain which hung from the pole and knocked over the skittles. This was a good game for home entertainment. Also, Jack had a large billiard table, complete with balls and cues. We would place the dining room table cornerwise in the large living room, and extend all the leaves, to support this billiard table and give plenty of elbow room for the players and their cues. This was a great pastime for Jack and his friends.

I had bought two pairs of real kid leather boxing gloves (intended for lightweight boxers) for Ivan, who was having lessons from my nephew in the police force; now he was busy demonstrating how he was going to teach this young soldier to box! Jack was proposing to have a game of billiards with our visitor, and everyone had something planned for him except for Pearl, who was keeping very silent; she was a rather shy teenager now.

Her Aunty Evelyn said, 'You can play the piano for him, Pearl, and we'll all sing!'

'And Mammy's contribution will be nice home cooking for him,' said Ivor. 'I'm sure he'll appreciate that after army food!'

'And as he's an English boy, he will especially enjoy Ray's welsh cakes,' agreed Evelyn's mother.

'Well now,' I said, 'I think it's time you children went to bed. You've all got to be up early in the morning.' (Evelyn had already put baby John and her niece Patsy to bed.)

I took Ivan up to bed, and we passed the soldier's room on the way; as we did so, I noticed something, and I told Ivan, 'Take off your clothes quickly, and jump into bed. I'll be back in a minute to hear you say your prayers.' Then I left him and ran swiftly down the two flights of stairs to the basement, where I hurriedly disconnected the wireless set, and told the others that every bit of our conversation had been overheard by the young soldier, as the headphones on the bedrail had picked up our voices and relayed them to him!

After this practically every fortnight we would have one young man leaving us and going back to camp while another arrived from somewhere up in England. Each soldier brought his emergency ration card with him, for a fortnight's rations, but board, lodging, food and entertainment were given by us, free, to every young man who came. On the morning when each young soldier left to go back to his barracks, I would place a ten shilling note in the breast pocket of his coat, for him to buy himself a drink on the way back. I would also give him a packet of sandwiches to eat on the train, and a little parcel of corned beef pasties and welsh (bakestone) cakes, to share with his mates when he returned to barracks.

I can't describe all the boys who came to us, but one day I had a telegram from the organisers of the scheme asking me if I would accept a young Air Force man, a Sergeant Da Silva, who was a Maori. 'He will be coloured,' Evelyn and her mother told me. 'Are you willing to take a coloured man?'

'If he's white enough to fight for Britain, he's white enough to have our hospitality,' I said.

So I replied to the telegram, saying I would be delighted. In due course another telegram arrived, telling me to meet Sergeant Da Silva at Nantyfyllon Station at 7 p.m. As it was getting very near that time when the message arrived, and we knew that this young man from New Zealand would never find his way from Nanty Station to our house by himself, my husband and I put on our coats and hats (because it was a bitterly cold winter night) and walked to "Nanty" in the blackout. The other soldiers had all come during daylight.

Ivor and I got there before the train arrived, and waited for our soldier boy to alight from a carriage. We watched the barrier, but no soldier appeared, and we became rather anxious. My husband asked the ticket collector at the barrier if anyone who could be a soldier from New Zealand had passed him, but he replied, 'No man in uniform has handed me a ticket.'

Then the station master said, 'He's probably gone up on the train to Caerau. I'll phone the station, and hold him there for you.' We left Nantyfyllon Station as quickly as we could, and made our way up to Caerau Station, two miles up the valley, only to be faced with the same situation—no such person had passed the barrier. I described him to the station staff as if he were an Australian soldier—tall, and wearing a large soft hat, with a New Zealand badge pinned to the upturned side of the hat, but I was still assured that no soldier had got off the train. So then I asked the station master if he would watch for the train on its return from the terminus in Abergwynfi, and if the soldier was still on it, direct him to my home; the station master promised that he would watch every carriage and see that the young man came safely down.

Ivor and I hurried home, going down the lane to our side entrance. We had left Pearl in charge until our return, and when we got into the house, there, to our very great surprise, sitting in front of a roaring fire, was a young man whom Pearl introduced as Sergeant George Da Silva. He told us that he had got off at Nantyfyllon Station, and then enquired his way up to the house.

We realised by his height—no more than five-foot-two—why we had failed to recognise him; we had been looking for a tall, Australian-type soldier, but this little boy of just eighteen years old had slipped through the barrier unnoticed.

'Surely you are too young to be a sergeant in the Air Force?' I said to him.

'Yes,' he replied, with great honesty, 'but I was desperate to get away to come to Britain, so I lied about my age. They think I am twenty, but I'm only eighteen.'

I asked Pearl why she had been trying to roast our guest to death with that great fire, because I could see that the heat was a bit much for the boy, and Pearl explained, 'Well, you know how cold *we* were when we came back from Australia, and we arrived during a heat wave. So I thought he would be feeling the cold even more, because it's winter now. I wanted to thaw him out.'

The young sergeant had a very bad cough, I noticed, and his chest was very bad, so I guessed that Lady Frances Rider and Miss Fry had sent him down on sick leave.

'How long are you staying with us, George?' I asked him.

'I've been given two week's leave,' he answered.

'Well,' I said, 'we've got to get that old chest and cough cured before you go, so I'm going to forget that you are a sergeant in the Air Force and treat you as if you were my son Jack, with a bad chest and a cough, because I know that's what your mother would want me to do.'

We had no electric blankets in those days—there *were*

177

none—and we couldn't buy rubber hot water bottles, as all such materials were needed for defence, so I popped some bricks into the hot oven at the side of the grate so that I could use them for his bed; they would retain their heat for hours. I had a double bed and a single bed in the big room that I used for my soldier guests, so I told George, 'I was going to give you the single bed, but I feel you will need to be kept warm during the night, so I'm going to put you in with Jack in the double bed. Do you mind that, George? Or would you prefer the single bed?'

'At home I share with my brother,' he said, 'So if Jack doesn't mind, I would really rather share with him.'

When the bricks were thoroughly heated through, they were wrapped individually, each in a piece of flannel, and put in the bed to warm it, before the boys went up. Then, when they went to bed, they could move the bricks down to the bottom of the bed, by their feet, and lie on the part that had just been warmed.

'Now don't be alarmed if you see me coming into the bedroom during the night,' I told George and Jack. 'I shall rub your chest, George, before I go to bed, then I'll probably come in during the night, to see that you're keeping warm.'

Before I went into my own room that night, I went into the boys' room, expecting to see the two of them back to back in the middle of the bed, keeping each other warm. To my surprise, I found Jack sleeping in his usual place, while George had drawn himself over to the furthest side of the bed, right against the wall. Although there were plenty of good bedclothes and a warm eiderdown on the bed, it was bitterly cold outside, so after rubbing George's chest and back with camphorated oil, rubbing it well in and following it with a dose of cough mixture, I said to the boy, 'What is this big gap doing in between you two, letting all the cold air into your backs? George, leave that wall alone, and come back to the middle of the bed!'

'George replied, very humbly, 'I thought Jack might object, because he is white and my skin is coloured.'

To this I said, 'Do you think that if Jack was going to object to you sleeping with him, I would have let you come to live with us and be upset? The colour of the skin doesn't make a scrap of difference, it's the man underneath that matters, and you two are both equal beneath your skins. So put your backs together and keep warm! I want that chest better before you go back to barracks.'

178

I emphasized this point very strongly, and several times during the night I crept into the boy's room to make sure they were well covered and keeping nice and warm.

It didn't take George long to call me "Mam" and my husband "Dad". No-one had suggested this to him, it simply showed that he was very much at home with us. He would go down to my mother's house too, at Number 103 Tonna Road, and spend time with her and Dai, and he called them "Gran" and "Grampa". He crept into our hearts and we all loved him. (I think he must have met with some opposition to his colour before he came to our house, and this made him feel a little apprehensive on the day of his arrival, but we soon got rid of that feeling.)

On the Saturday when he was leaving us to go back to camp, he wasn't willing to take my usual gift of ten shillings, but I insisted. He gladly accepted the sandwiches to eat on the train, though, and my little parcel of food for him to share with his fellow-soldiers when he got back. The application of camphorated oil, applied night and morning, along with the cough mixture, had completely cleared his cough and chest, and he was quite fit to return.

Jack went with him to Cardiff to see him off, and when Jack got back, he told us that George had tears in his eyes when he said goodbye.

'I feel more homesick today, leaving your home,' he told Jack, 'than I did when I left New Zealand. I have a Mam and a Dad, two brothers and a sister, and a Gran and Grampa there, but I came here and found two brothers and a sister, a Mam and Dad, and a Gran and Grampa along with them! I shall miss you all very much. Can I come again, do you think, Jack?'

'Certainly, George,' Jack said. 'And I'm speaking for all my family—you'll always be welcome.'

From that day on, George Da Silva became our own "adopted" son. We corresponded and sent him food parcels, and he spent all his leave with us. He did this for the remaining two years of the war, often spending weekends with us as well, and in due course he applied for a transfer to an army air camp in Wales from which he could often visit us.

One day, some months after his first visit to us, his first words when he walked in were, 'Mam, I've got a present for you.'

He handed me a small, wrapped-up packet, and I said, 'What is it, George? You shouldn't spent your money on a present for me.'

179

'I have won my first "Wing", Mam,' he said, 'and I'm giving it to you.'

I opened the packet, and my eyes filled with tears. I knew what the first "Wing" meant to an Air Force man, it was something sacred, and here he was, giving his to me.

'George,' I said, 'this belongs to your real Mam and Dad in New Zealand. Send it to them—it will make them very proud of you.'

'No, Mam,' he told me. 'You are my Mam now, in this country, and I want you to have it.'

I couldn't refuse any longer. 'I will treasure this all my life,' I said. Later I bought a piece of red velvet and embroidered the black and white "Wing" onto it, then embroidered the letters "SERGEANT DA SILVA" above it, and added the date on which he won it. Lastly I framed the piece of velvet and kept it as a treasured possession.

George always called every Wednesday "Mam's Day", because that was the day on which we used to go out together to visit my sister Violet, who was still living down in Bridgend. We often attracted great curiosity in passers-by as we walked through the Bridgend bus station and the crowded streets of the town; they stared at us in surprise as they saw us walking arm-in-arm and heard George addressing me as "Mam"—in those days it was a remarkable sight, a Welsh mother with a Maori son!

TWENTY SIX

Springtime came to Caerau once more, and with so many people coming back and forth to my basement, it occurred to me that it would be nice to have a lawn, so that people could sit out on it in deckchairs in the summer.

Ivor's illhealth meant that we would never be using the bakehouse again, and when there was an appeal for everyone to give any spare iron to help the war effort, Ivor had dismantled the big ovens and handed them over; he had taken the wheels off all the trolleys, too, and every other bit of iron we could find was also given to help the war effort.

At one time Jack and his friends had had a great deal of fun in the old bakehouse. They had turned it into a "Pirates' Den" when they were little boys, and painted big white skulls and crossbones all over it, and the old place had given them a great many years of pleasure and play, with all of them dressed up as pirates, plotting and planning their games. Now, though, Jack was an apprentice and had a girlfriend, and he and his pals had no further use for the building, so I decided that our house would be healthier if we took down the bakehouse and had a garden instead, giving more light and air to the basement.

My husband employed a few out-of-work men to take the bakehouse building down, and when it was demolished, all the tiles that had come off the roof were stacked away for later use on our house. The absence of the bakehouse left a large open space with a flagged floor, so we took the flagstones up and carried earth from the bank of the river to fill in the foundations of the demolished building. By the time Summer arrived, we had a lovely lawn, with a beautiful flower border.

All this made a great improvement to living in the basement, where we now had plenty of light and air, and it was extremely pleasant, although there was one snag to taking down the bakehouse that we had overlooked. The property was leasehold, and by law the bakehouse would have to be replaced at the end of the ninety-nine year lease. There was only one thing to do; we bought the freehold, and then we had no further problems, we could sit back and enjoy the beauty and comfort of our nice garden.

*   *   *

Now at last the war was coming to a close. Evelyn and her family had gone back to their homes in Mitcham, but I could look forward to more visitors. My sister Emily had written from Australia to tell me that many of the young men from Northampton (the little bush town we had sometimes visited when we lived out in the wilds of Western Australia), had joined up at the beginning of the war. Emily had given them my address in Wales, hoping that they would have an opportunity to visit us while they were in Britain.

However, because these men had been brought up in a bush environment and were familiar with jungle-type conditions, they had been sent to New Guinea, where they were engaged in jungle warfare. Eventually news had come that they had been captured and held as prisoners of war. Now, Emily explained, the British had been able to recapture New Guinea and release all the prisoners, and the Northampton boys were among the vast number of those who were being brought back to England on troop ships, to recuperate. Any repatriated prisoner of war who had an address in this country could get a free rail warrant to go and stay at that address for an unlimited time, and so my home was invaded by these repatriated Australians. They were very welcome guests.

Until George Da Silva came, I had only been able to give hospitality to British troops. No Dominion troops had been sent, and I did not offer hospitality to American soldiers because they were very well paid by their own American government, and could afford to pay for anything they wanted. British and Dominion troops, however, were very poorly paid, and had no money to pay for accommodation, so they could only go home to their families (if they had a family) when they were on leave, or else stay in their barracks.

Some of the Australians who came to stay with me found girlfriends in the valleys, whom they married; these were then able to stay with their fiancées' or wives' families, so I had more room

182

and more time to give to other Aussies. There were two men in particular, Sid Francis and Ted White, who spent a long time in our home. They were in their forties, and in a very bad way. They told me that some of their injuries had been self-inflicted, to prevent them from being forced to help the enemy in New Guinea.

I had arranged with my doctors that they would attend all the repatriated prisoners who came to my house, and they did this free of charge. They told me that there were so many things wrong with Sid Francis and Ted White that they didn't know where to start to put things right, but they did what they could, and cleaned the sand and grit out of Ted White's eyes—this mess had been causing him a lot of pain. Several times they put Ted's knees back into joint; they had both been so badly damaged that they couldn't stop in position. The doctors told Ted and Sid that when they were sent back to Australia to be demobilised, they must sign themselves in at the first hospital they came to and stay there until the staff could, if possible, put their bodies together again.

All the Australians who came to me brought no money at all with them, but they all liked a drink, so Ivor would take them out every night to one or other of the local pubs in the valley. Immediately they entered a pub door, they would receive a tremendous welcome from all the local men, who would shower them with so many drinks that they wanted for nothing! The Australians were so impressed by the generosity of the people in Caerau that when they were notified that they were embarking for Australia and must return at once, they each and every one had the same thing to say to Ivor and me when we wished them "goodbye" at the station in Bridgend.

'We don't know what sort of welcome you had when you first came out to Australia,' they said, 'but we do know what sort of welcome you'll have, should you come back again!'

Ted White and Sid Francis begged us to return some time, if only so that they could return the kindness we had shown to all the Aussies. 'When you come back to Northampton,' they told us, 'there won't be a man, woman or child in the town or the surrounding bush, that won't be on Northampton Station to welcome you back. And we'll be leading the band!'

The Aussies corresponded with me for years, and to this day I still hear from some of the people in Australia. Sid Francis married, and his wife sent me some photographs of their children, but Ted White told his friends and relatives that he had left his heart in

183

Wales, and he couldn't settle back into the monotonous life of the bush. At last, in a fit of deep depression, he jumped down a deep well, and so, very sadly, ended his life. He was only about forty-five when he committed suicide.

My sister's eldest daughter, Beryl, the little girl who had been born in Ogmore Vale, was now married to the son of a farmer in Australia, and the farmer had set them up in a model farm of their own. Soon after the death of my little baby girl, Beryl had given birth to a baby girl of her own, and had named her Elaine Margaret after my baby. The family supplied me regularly with photographs of this little Elaine, who was a very lovely child.

Now, while he was with me in Wales, Sid Francis had told me that he was engaged to my sister's second daughter, Edna, who was serving in the Australian Army, but hadn't been sent overseas. When Sid and Ted White had been about to return to Australia, we had given them many souvenirs to take back to their relations and friends, and as Sid was betrothed to Edna (although I thought he was many years too old for my young niece), I entrusted to him a gift for little Elaine. It was a beautiful necklace of seed pearls, designed especially for a small child.

I asked Sid to be sure to take care of this necklace and give it to Beryl's little one personally, from me, and he assured me that he would do so, but unfortunately he was not able to keep his promise; I found out years later that the child had never received the pearls. Unluckily, when Sid arrived back home, he found that Edna was engaged to somebody else, and perhaps it was because of this and his anger and disappointment that the necklace was never handed over.

There was a strange coincidence about my Elaine and Beryl's little Elaine. When my baby died, the doctors told me that I shouldn't grieve for the child, as it was a blessing that she had been taken there and then, when still a baby. Her tiny heart and liver were in such a bad state what she would have been a little invalid in a corner all through her childhood, and could only have been taken about in a specially built carriage. They told me that it was possible she might have lived for fourteen years, or until she was twenty-one at the very longest. And although it was hard to part with her as a baby, it would have been much harder to part with a young lady of twenty-one, after all those years in what was called a "bath chair".

Now, little Elaine Robb in Australia was a beautiful, healthy child until she reached the age of eight, and then she developed the same symptoms that had killed my own little girl. I thought the heat of Australia might be too much for her, so I volunteered to care for her if her parents were prepared to send her to me, to see if our much cooler climate would turn out to be more suitable. However Beryl and her husband couldn't bear to part with their beautiful child, and so they sold their farm in the bush and bought a bungalow in Geraldton, hoping that the sea air and the cooler temperatures would be kinder to their "little piece of Dresden china", as they called her.

Elaine Robb was a very happy little girl, even though she was constantly in and out of hospital. It was hoped that she would out-grow her delicate state of heath as she got older, and on her twenty-first birthday they gave a ball for her. (Her parents were comfortably off, and they could afford to give her the best of everything.) Photographs were taken at the ball, and a beautiful one, of Elaine in her lovely white ballgown, was sent to me. She made a charming little picture, but together with the photograph, when it arrived in the post, was the sad ending of the story.

After the ball Elaine retired to bed, and her mother sat at the foot of the bed while her daughter told her what a wonderful time she'd had at her party, with the young doctor she'd had as her escort. Beryl was surprised that although it was a warm night, Elaine said she was feeling cold, but she went to the store-cupboard and brought out an eiderdown that she then wrapped around the girl in bed. She covered her up, and said, 'Go to sleep. You're tired and excited. I'm glad you've had such a wonderful birthday, but I'll leave you now, and we'll take more about it in the morning when you are less tired.'

But when Beryl went into Elaine's room the following morning to call her for breakfast, she found her little girl was dead. She had not survived one day after her twenty-first birthday. Poor Beryl was grief-stricken.

It was very strange to think that of the five children my mother had reared, and all the grandchildren and great-grandchildren she had, at home and abroad, these two little Elaines, mine and Beryl's, had died of the same complaint in two different countries. My little girl could only have lived, so it was said, until she was twenty-one, and now this other Elaine had been taken at exactly that age.

I felt as if I were losing my own little girl for a second time when

I read the news. I was terribly upset at her death, and although many years have passed since then, her mother has never got over the shock of finding her precious, lovely, young daughter dead in bed.

After the Aussies had all gone back home to their native land, George Da Silva came again, on his next leave, and when I next took Ivan down for his singing lesson, I told his music master and the master's sister, my friend Maud, about George. At that, they said, 'Shall we make a party for him, here in our house? We'd love to hold one, to make him welcome, and we could call some of our friends and neighbours in to meet him.'

So it was arranged, and Maud and Sid Bowen sent out invitation cards to their friends, to ask them to come to a party being held in honour of our guest, Sergeant Da Silva. The party was timed to take place just a few days before George was due to return to his base, and it turned out to be a really lovely affair, which George said he thoroughly enjoyed, particularly meeting so many new people. Among those present was the inspector from the Ministry of Food who had threatened to "get" me one day because I refused to assist him in a possible law case against some of my neighbours in Tonna Road. He was there with his wife, but no reference at all was made to past conflicts; we all enjoyed ourselves and the past was forgotten. We were a gay, happy crowd, making joyful memories for George to take home with him to New Zealand at some time in the future.

TWENTY SEVEN

It was now nearing the fourth Christmas of the war. I had no soldiers in the house, only my usual evacuees, Evelyn, her mother and the two children, and at last I had time to look around and count the damage done to my home and my bank account by all the people I'd had to provide for and keep during the war.

There was very little to sell in the shops at that time, after the rations had been distributed, and the rations themselves were so small that there was very little profit to be made in business. For years now fresh eggs had been replaced by dehydrated ones, which at first we had found to be extremely unpleasant to the taste, but now they were just something to eat. We were glad of anything, even the stinging nettles did not grow fast enough for us because we ate those in place of cabbage! Dandelion leaves, too, became a treasure; we would cut them up and soak them in vinegar, then eat them with margarine. (Anything to push the marge down!)

Oranges and bananas we hadn't tasted for years. We would occasionally have an allocation from our fruiterer, but to obtain fruit you had to produce "Baby Ration" cards, and then there would only be one orange or one banana per baby book, per allocation; and sometimes the fruiterer would not be able to supply the full allocation to my shop (the full allocation would perhaps be six oranges or six bananas.) The only thing we could do if this happened would be to show the customers the amount allowed to me and ask which, if any, would be willing to wait for the next allocation—which might come in a week, but could also take as long as a month.

The parents or the lucky baby who would be getting his or her oranges or bananas would then have the book or books stamped by us with the date, to make sure that we knew who had, or had not, had their fruit. Nestlé Milk was also supplied only to babies, as there was not enough to distribute to adults as well, and there were many other similar foodstuffs which were only distributed to

187

babies. It was left to the discretion of the shopkeeper to distribute these things to the best of his or her ability.

Before my little Elaine was born, I had craved for an orange, but of course I had not been able to have one, and when the child was born, she was putting her tongue out as if craving for something. Whether it was just an "old wives" tale or not, the nurse said it was because I had been craving for something during my pregnancy, and I knew it must be that orange. However I had still not tasted an orange in all those years. Then, one night, a local fruiterer came in through my side entrance and into the kitchen where I was resting; he had a sack on his back and a broad grin on his face.

'I've brought you a present, Mrs. Webb,' he announced. 'I've got some oranges for you.' With this he put a quarter of a sack of oranges down on the floor, by my feet.

I thought this would make a lovely contribution to our Christmas comforts, and I asked, 'Is this a special allocation for us?'

'No, it's a little present for you,' he replied. 'On the Q.T.'

My mood changed when I heard this, and I said, 'And what do you want for these—on the Q.T.?'

He said, 'Well, I thought we could make a little swap. You give me some sugar from your ice-cream allocation sugar, and I'll give you these oranges.'

I looked him straight in the face, and said, 'How many little babies have you robbed to bring me these?'

The man thought I was joking, and he laughed. 'I thought you'd be glad to have them,' he said.

'Yes,' I said. 'I would be very glad to have them if I was entitled to them, but you just take them back to the little babies who are being deprived of them—I wouldn't touch these oranges with a barge pole! We've had four years of war, and in all this time, I've never yet stooped to black marketing, and I don't intend to let myself be tempted by you, however much I would like an orange! And as for ice-cream sugar, I have a very good allocation—two hundredweight a month—and a good allocation of margarine, and I don't use it all every month in ice-cream, but neither do I black market it. I have used a great deal of it throughout this war to feed and care for homeless people, and to give comfort and home-cooking to all the soldiers that have visited my home. I certainly won't give any sugar to you, you greedy creature.

Pick up your oranges and get out of my house at once. The war won't last for ever, but I will be able to hold my head up when it's over. Can you say that about yourself?'

I opened the door for him to leave, showing my contempt by slamming it after him.

I had always been a thrifty person, and I didn't drink or smoke or gamble, or even go to any place of entertainment through all those years of war. I called any spare bit of money my pocket money, and I would put that little bit away for a rainy day, as the expression goes. Now the "rainy day" had come and gone, in caring for all those soldiers, and I had no money to fall back on. Although my husband had worked for quite some time in the colliery and then in the arsenal, his only contribution to the upkeep of our home was to pay the rates and the electricity bill, but I knew that he wasn't squandering his money, because his one fear, knowing of his illness, was that he would die prematurely, and so he was making provision for our old age. However, because of this, I knew I would receive no financial help from Ivor.

Still, my children and I had had nothing new in the way of clothing for several years, and we badly needed new winter clothing, while the children had outgrown many of their outer garments. My annual check-up on my sheets found many of them badly torn, though I could overcome this problem with fresh patches, and my towels were also very worn and would have to be patched so that they would last longer. However the children's clothes could not wait, so I had to find some way of making money.

At that particular time no nice toys for little girls seemed to be coming into the shops; the only toys available were war toys—soldiers and so on. In my shop I had an empty tomato basket, and this gave me an idea. I saw in my mind's eye how it would look if it was decorated and made into a doll's cot. So after the shop had closed in the evening, I took this wooden basket (which was about two feet in length and twelve inches in width, with a solid base) and carried it downstairs, where I used sandpaper to make sure there would be no splinters in the wood to injure a small child's hands.

As my husband was a handy man about the house, there were always pieces of spare wood to be found in our home, so I selected

189

four pieces of about the same length, and with my son's fretwork saw, I trimmed the edges to make them stand firmly, as these were to be the legs of the cot. Then I took two of the legs, crossed them, and secured them with some thin carpenter's nails; I did the same to the other two legs, and then painted them all. Next I fixed these legs to the four corners of the cot, and lined the inside with some remnants, from the market, of the satin used for lining jackets and coats. I then took a long piece of material, the same colour as the lining (which was pink) and pleated it all around the outside of the cot, to hang down low.

At the head of the cot, in the centre, I put a piece of thin pliable wood which I could bend so that it was suspended over the cot, ready to support a canopy. I then draped this wood with a piece of the same material, and secured it at both sides, about five inches down at the head of the cot. After that I frilled and draped a remnant of fine lace curtain over the canopy, and made white ribbon bows, one at the centre, over the canopy, and one on either side where the lace curtain met the material. The next job was to make a mattress and a little pillow for the cot from a piece of white material, while a piece of the satin lining, quilted, made an effective eiderdown. I edged the pillow with lace, leaving the completed cot ready for display in my shop window.

However an empty cot was no good without a doll in it, and since I had not been able to obtain any dolls for my shop in recent years, I made a rag doll with my sewing machine, stuffed it, and painted eyes, nose and mouth on it for a face, using strands of wool for the hair. Lastly I made a little lace bonnet and a white nightdress, and placed the doll under the pink quilted eiderdown.

I took the doll's cot and put it on display in the centre of the "toy window" in the shop, It was late in the night by this time, so I would have to wait patiently to see what effect it would have on the public in the morning. When I opened the shop door the next day, to let the schoolchildren in, I found a policeman waiting on the doorstep. He said, 'Mrs. Webb, that's a beautiful doll's cot you've got in the window. How much does it cost?'

'One pound, five shillings (£1.25),' I replied.

'I've got two little girls,' he said. 'Do you think you could have another one for me? I'd like them to have one each. I think this cot is really beautiful.'

'It is home-made,' I told him. 'I made it myself.'

I showed him the cot, and he studied it and exclaimed that it was very well made, and he would certainly want another one.

'While the other one is being made for you,' I said, 'do you mind if I leave this one on display with a "Sold" ticket on it, so that I can take orders?'

The policeman said he didn't mind at all, and so the cot was left in the window. I ended up with so many orders for the cots that it was necessary for me to go to Maesteg Market, where the fruiterer promised to keep all the empty baskets for me for free, as he had lots and was glad to be rid of them.

I bought enough material remnants of various colours and lace curtain remnants (all quite cheap) to supply all the orders that came into the shop for my "Dolls in Cots", and in the end I made enough money from this little venture to rig out my three children in a new winter outfit each—winter coat, shoes, stockings, everything, including warm winter gloves. I had never had so much money to call my own in my entire life! Every rag doll and cot I made brought in, after deducting the cost of the materials, a profit of a pound.

One day, while I was still being kept busy making the dolls and the cots, a soldier in uniform came into the shop. He lived at the bottom of Tonna Road, and he was on leave from the front line at the time. He told me he was desperate to buy a doll's pram, as he had tried in Swansea, Bridgend and Cardiff, and had failed to get one anywhere.

'Could you make a doll's pram for me, I wonder?' he asked. 'Since you make these lovely cots?'

I told him that this was out of the question. A pram would require wheels and axles, and I couldn't possibly make anything like a perambulator. Anyway, there was no metal about, it had all been taken for use in the war effort.

At that, the man said, 'All my little girl is talking about is a "dolly pram". And I'm going back tomorrow. She'll be a bitterly disappointed child on Christmas morning if she hasn't got her pram. I can't bear to go back without having got her one.'

He seemed so dejected, and I thought of Pearl's bassinette doll's pram which had became her souvenir of her childhood in Australia. She loved that pram.

'Are you going back to the firing line?' I asked the soldier.

'Yes,' he said.

I visualised him on the battle-field on Christmas Day, in all the mud and cold, thinking of his little girl's disappointment and tears, and a terrible sense of guilt possessed me, because I had a pram wrapped up in a cloth on top of the wardrobe in my bedroom. (Though to me this doll's pram was a priceless treasure.) I didn't worry about the little girl being disappointed, as I knew there would be thousands of little girls disappointed on Christmas morning, and my own children had gone without many times during the years of war. But I did worry about this young father. He was going back to the front line, perhaps to be killed and never see his little daughter again, and that pram on top of my wardrobe could at least give him a little comfort on Christmas Day if he thought his little girl was happy. I asked him if he could come back later in the evening, and I would see if something could possibly be arranged after I had had a word with my daughter.

When Pearl came home, I told her about the soldier. I didn't feel at all happy about parting with the pram, nor did Pearl, especially as this man and his family had lived in the street for years and never been customers of mine. I had to admit to myself that I was wishing he hadn't come in now, and Pearl was very loath to part with her pram, but we decided that the man, like so many more boys from our street, was suffering hardship and danger for King and Country, and if they could sacrifice for us, we should sacrifice for them. So when the soldier came back in the evening, I showed him the bassinette.

He was absolutely overjoyed, and couldn't believe his good fortune. It was quite a large bassinette, and he offered to pay me for it. I said, 'I couldn't put a price on it, so I'll give it to you as a present.'

The soldier went back to the front line, but came back safely after the war, and his daughter, who is now a married woman with children of her own, ironically enough lives next door to my daughter Pearl.

TWENTY EIGHT

It was June, 1945, and that wonderful day—VE Day—was near at hand. Mr. Will Griffiths was still calling at our house for his morning cup of coffee and a chat with Ivor, who wasn't working now. He had only been working in the arsenal for a short time when he collapsed on the road, and his lung condition was discovered. Ivor had now been made exempt from all National Service work.

Will called in several times a day on his way to and from school, and he would give us a running commentary on how much money the small street that he lived in had collected in anticipation of V.E. Day. They had amassed more than a hundred pounds in a house-to-house collection taken each week. Indeed, it seemed that every street in the valley had a large sum of money in preparation for this celebration—all except Tonna Road, which had collected nothing at all. Tonna Road was a long street, with approximately two hundred children living in it, yet no-one had made any attempt to prepare for a party.

I had often brought up the subject, with the mothers when they came into my shop, and had suggested that they did something about organizing a street party, and many a time I had heard mothers complaining that nobody was interested in doing something for the children in Tonna Road. But it was always the same. Each one was waiting for someone else to make the move.

On the eve of V.E. Day Will was at our house, still talking about the wonderful time they were going to have in Magazine Street the next day, and how beautifully their street had been decorated with bunting and flags. I felt great pity for the little children of Tonna Road, who would be deprived of this special joy, and I looked at the clock. It was twelve midnight, and normally, if Will hadn't been there, we would have been in bed. But I made up my mind, there and then, that although the time was short, and we'd made no preparations, something had to be done for Tonna Road.

193

I went out the back with a chair and a sweeping brush and climbed on the chair. Then I banged on the currugated iron roof of my next-door-neighbour's toilet with the brush. As it happened, Mrs. Thomas was also up late that particular night, and she came down her garden to ask what I wanted.

'You know the celebrations are tomorrow,' I said. 'Isn't it a shame that no-one has done anything for our street? Are you willing to stay up all night tonight and help me do something?'

'Yes, certainly, Mrs. Webb,' she agreed. 'Anything you like.'

Her enthusiasm encouraged me, so I told her, 'Well, you go down and ask Norah Hurley to come up. I don't expect they've gone to bed, they're usually up late. Tell Norah that I want her help.'

So Mrs. Thomas went down the street and brought back Mrs. Norah Hurley, a young mother with schoolchildren.

'What do you want me to do, Mrs. Webb?' asked Norah, willingly.

'You make good welsh cakes, Norah,' I said. 'Would you be prepared to stay up all night, making them for a party in the street tomorrow, if I supply you with the ingredients?'

'Yes,' she replied. 'I would be delighted.' So I gave her as much ice-cream sugar and margarine as I knew she would need, and all the flour and dehydrated eggs that she required, and she spent all that night cooking cakes on her bakestone. I told her that we needed a large quantity, as there would be a lot of children to cater for.

Mrs. Thomas and I spent the whole night in my kitchen, making jellies and cakes, and early the next morning Mrs. Thomas went out to collect four of the neighbours, Mrs. Hurley Senior, Mrs. Hannah Lewis, and two other ladies whose names I have forgotten. I told them that I would like them to take a big shopping bag and go from door to door in Tonna Road, asking for either a contribution in money or a piece of whatever they could spare of "off the ration" food. The response was terrific. As I couldn't afford to shoulder the expense of the whole party, I said we would have to have money to pay for all the goods we were taking from my shop, and I put five pounds into the kitty to give it a start. I also told the other that I would make all the ice-cream free, and that would also be my contribution.

As soon as the men of the street knew what was being done, I had no need to worry about helpers! They came to ask what they

194

could do to help, and I told them to go home, get their kitchen tables, and set them up in a line all the way along the street. Then they were to bring as many chairs and stools as they could, for the children to sit on. Meanwhile I told the mothers to hang any flags they had out of the windows, to decorate the street as much as possible.

Everyone was greatly excited. They were having a special treat they had not expected, and they all joined in the activities with great zeal. In a very short time the street was filled with pieces of paper, in all the pretty colours that people could find, strung out from one side of the road to the other on strings, as makeshift bunting! It caused roars of laughter when some women hung a line of washing across the street, singing, 'We're going to hang out the washing on the Siegfried Line, have you any dirty washing, Mother Dear?'

Now the children kept coming to me and asking, 'Mrs. Webb, what can we do?' Like everyone else they wanted to do something, but they were more of a hindrance than a help, so I hit on a plan to keep them off the street and out of my way.

'Go home,' I said, 'and get anything you can find for fancy dress. Decide what you want to be, then after you've had your tea, we'll have a carnival!'

(Although all the traffic had been diverted, there were still a few odd vehicles coming up the road now and then, and I was afraid that if we didn't keep them off the street, in the midst of the excitement, a child might be injured.)

I left the table arrangements to the many women helpers, each of whom brought her own tablecloths and laid the places. I went into the shop and cut up all the bread on my bacon slicing machine, while a team of women buttered it and made sandwiches from the tins of Spam that had been donated. We had also been given tins of fruit. By the time we had distributed all the cakes and other food on to the tables, they were groaning under the weight of it all!

Several of the local councillors came around, as they were doing a survey of all the street parties to see who had the best turnout, and they told us ours was the best street tea they had seen anywhere in the valley. So we told them that we had only organised it that morning.

The children tucked into the food with glee, and I think it must have been the first time in five years that those little tummies were fully satisfied. To finish their feast, they were all supplied with a big helping of ice-cream—then, when the children rose from the table, we were sure they could eat no more! As there was still a great deal of food left, the tables were cleared and then freshly set out for the adults.

In order to keep the children all together and keep the road clear, I sent each child who had been able to find something they could use as fancy dress, home to get their clothes, while I took those who had nothing into my basement. There I used an old Japanese kimono of my mother's to dress one little girl as a Japanese lady, complete with paper fan, and I used bath towels to make 'the Order of the Bath' and several other easy to make costumes so that everyone who wanted to could dress up.

Then I got each of the children to fetch a comb and piece of paper to cover it, and we formed a 'Comb Band', with the children all blowing through the combs and paper. I marched them all up to what we called the "Top of the Hill", which was a point a little beyond Tonna Road, and as they marched, they played on their combs all the marching songs they knew. After that we marched all the way down through Tonna Road to Nantyfyllon and back, to give the adults time to enjoy their hard-earned tea without having the children to worry them. I wanted everyone to have had their tea, ready for the little presentation I intended to make.

Before the party began, I had said, 'As we are celebrating the end of the war, we need a soldier.' The only soldier home at the time was Johnny Evans of Tonna David Farm (the farm over which the German parachutists had been dropped), who was on sick leave. As the farm was just behind Tonna Road, I sent two young boys up to ask him to come down in his uniform, because I needed to see him immediately. He came down with the boys, and I told him, 'We want you to be the guest of honour at the adults' party;' we put him to sit in a place of honour at the table.

Then before the people had quite finished eating, I brought the marching children back, and told them to stand quietly at the side of the road while I said a few words to Johnny Evans. I concluded my little speech by handing him a five pound note, the amount of surplus money left after the expenses had all been taken out of the amount collected that morning.

After this, the tables were cleared, and all of them except one were carried back into the houses from which they had come, while all the surplus food was put together on the one table remaining, making a "running buffet" for anyone who felt hungry during the evening's entertainment. Some men carried my piano from our sitting room, through the shop and out on to the pavement, then Jack and Pearl, who by this time were pretty accomplished pianists, took it in turns to play, and we had community singing and dancing all through the evening and well on into the night.

At about eleven or twelve o'clock that night, a tall, smart, military man stopped all the dancing and the noise by ringing a bell for silence. He was Mr. Jim Hurley, Senior, who had served all through the 1914-18 war, but was too old to serve in this second world war; though he had given one of his elder sons, who later died as a result of injuries sustained in battle.

By this time there was a tremendous crowd in the street; Mr. Hurley addressed us all, asking, 'Have you all had a marvellous time?' and everyone agreed unanimously that they had. Then Mr. Hurley went on to say, 'Well, you've got one woman to thank for all this, and I don't need to tell you who she is. It was midnight last night when she knocked on our doors and told us that something had to be done at once, so that all our children would not be disappointed. So give three cheers for Mrs. Webb the shop!'

But I didn't hear the cheering, I was fast asleep. Still, it was a rewarding end to a wonderful day.

The V.E. Day party really marked the end of the war for us in Caerau, but when V.J. Day came, marking the end of hostilities everywhere, I was in London, where we were staying with my aunt and uncle. We went up to the City to see the celebrations, and it seemed that night as if all the world was in London. Everyone was laughing and shouting, and it seemed that London had gone mad with happiness. Rich and poor, black and white, all mixed together, milling around rejoicing.

It was a night I shall never forget. I had never seen anything like it before. One minute I had my arms around the neck of a black man, the next I was being hugged by a Russian—he was so tall that he seemed to tower above me. There were soldiers there of every nationality, Australians, New Zealanders, Americans, Canadians, British Tommys, and we were all hugging and kissing one another. It was, for us that night, the end of the war that was to end all wars throughout the world.

197

We were all under the same old flag,
Brothers in arms were we;
One King and one Empire,
One flag and one desire.

England, Ireland, Scotland, Wales,
And comrades over the sea.